GINGERS
of
CAMBODIA, LAOS & VIETNAM

GINGERS
of
CAMBODIA, LAOS & VIETNAM

Jana Leong-Škorničková
&
Mark Newman

Singapore Botanic Gardens, National Parks Board

in association with
Royal Botanic Garden Edinburgh
&
Pha Tad Ke Botanical Garden

2015

Published by
Singapore Botanic Gardens, National Parks Board
1 Cluny Road, Singapore 259569
www.sbg.org.sg • www.nparks.gov.sg
Tel: 65-64717361 • Fax: 65-64737983

in association with
Royal Botanic Garden Edinburgh
20A Inverleith Row, Edinburgh EH3 5LR
Scotland, United Kingdom
www.rbge.ac.uk

and
Pha Tad Ke Botanical Garden
Ban Wat That, PO Box 959, 06000 Luang Prabang
Lao P.D.R.
www.pha-tad-ke.com

*First published in August 2015 with the generous support of Mr Tan Jiew Hoe
in Singapore, administered through the Garden City Fund.*

ISBN: 978-981-09-6380-4

Design: Jana Leong-Škorničková & Rik Gadella
Layout and print: Oxford Graphic Printers Pte Ltd
Printed in Singapore in 2.200 copies

Frontispiece: *Curcuma rhabdota*, drawn by Sandy Ross Sykes.

Curcuma alismatifolia.

Zingiber sp.

CONTENTS

Zingiber pellitum.

Foreword

The biodiversity of Cambodia, Laos and Vietnam, often referred to as Indochina, is still poorly known with one of the lowest collection densities in SE Asia yet, with every passing year, it becomes clear that the richness of this region far surpasses initial estimates, some amazing discoveries being made in recent years. A multitude of new species, including large mammals, strange amphibians and plants belonging to new and endemic genera, has been discovered in this region. Gingers, being one of the most charismatic yet taxonomically notoriously difficult plant groups, are no exception. Many have been described as new to science or recorded for the first time in recent years, while even more may still await discovery.

Gingers are present in almost every habitat in Cambodia, Laos and Vietnam. They can be found from the lowlands to the highest peaks, in all the various forest types. In urbanised areas, numerous ginger species also play important roles in the daily lives of the people. It is hard to find a local market which does not sell at least a few types of ginger, whether for food or medicinal purposes, and many of the local minorities still rely heavily on wild-collected gingers to treat various ailments; many of these gingers are not yet formally described. Others are used for ornamental purposes and some of them hold yet unlocked economical potential for these countries.

While there has been fairly good coverage of similar pictorial books featuring *Gingers of Peninsular Malaysia and Singapore*, *Gingers of Thailand*, *Gingers of China* and, most recently, *A guide to the gingers of Borneo*, there are virtually no resources to the gingers of Cambodia, Laos and Vietnam. This book is therefore a long-awaited and welcome attempt to close this knowledge gap.

Many gingers are locally endemic and found only in primary vegetation. This makes them very vulnerable to various changes connected with rapid urbanisation and development of these countries. I am proud to sponsor this book which I hope will promote an interest in further studies of the flora and intensify conservation efforts in these countries.

Mr Tan Jiew Hoe
President of the Singapore Gardening Society

Zingiber jiewhoei, a species endemic to Laos, was named in honour of Mr Tan Jiew Hoe for his continuous contributions towards ginger research.

Preface

The latest comprehensive treatment of gingers in Cambodia, Laos and Vietnam, compiled by French botanist François Gagnepain, is more than a century old. When we started to working in this region, fewer than a hundred ginger species were recorded in Cambodia, Laos and Vietnam. After a few field trips which explored only a fraction of the forests, it became obvious that the diversity of the family is far greater than we had expected. We estimate that at least 300–400 species will eventually be recognised in this region. Many of these will be new records of species occurring in neighbouring countries, particularly Thailand and China, while others represent yet undescribed species, new to science. The identities of several species described in the early years and often based on dried herbarium material is also not yet clear, requiring new flowering collections from their type localities, some of which have changed radically since plants were originally collected there.

Given the overwhelming biodiversity of this region and our still limited knowledge of the flora in Cambodia, Laos and Vietnam, this book is by no means comprehensive. We have tried our best to illustrate a range of species of each genus to allow readers to identify plants to generic level, and to represent some of the species most commonly encountered in these three countries. About 30 new species mainly from Vietnam are currently being described. Some of these are already featured in this book and can be recognised by their names in quotation marks. These will be validly published in our research papers in the near future.

We have divided this book into two parts. The introductory part, consisting of 11 chapters, introduces readers to the various aspects of the region, to the intriguing world of gingers and their relatives, their morphology, current classification, ecology and conservation. The second part of the book then features all 18 genera so far recorded from Cambodia, Laos and Vietnam. Each of these richly illustrated generic chapters contains basic diagnostic characters and a generic description, information on habitat, number of species worldwide and within Cambodia, Laos and Vietnam, uses and, in taxonomically complicated genera, also some notes.

We hope you enjoy reading this book as much as we have enjoyed researching and writing it.

Jana Leong-Škorničková & Mark Newman

Tad Sa Leyi waterfall, northern Laos.

Acknowledgements

Production of this book would not have been possible without generous funding by Mr Tan Jiew Hoe.

Many of the specimens and photographs used in writing this book were gathered during Sud Expert Plantes project 350, entitled *Botanical study of the family Zingiberaceae in Indochina (Cambodia, Laos and Vietnam)* (http://www.sud-expert-plantes.ird.fr/projets/dossier_350). We gratefully acknowledge the funding we received from Sud Expert Plantes which was a programme funded by the French government. Jérôme Millet was the administrator of SEP in Laos. His contribution towards the running of SEP project 350 was invaluable. For help in organising and partaking in fieldwork in Cambodia, we thank Mme Yok Lin and Mr Ly Viboth; in Laos Dr Lammai Phiphakkhavong and Dr Vichith Lamxay; and in Viet Nam Professor Trần Triết (principal investigator of SEP project 350), Prof. Lê Công Kiệt and Mr Trần Hữu Đăng.

Fieldwork in Laos was supported by the Biotechnology and Ecology Institute in Vientiane (Mrs Somsanith Bouamanivong), Pha Tad Ke Botanic Gardens (Mr Rik Gadella, Mr Keooudone Souvannakhoummane, Mr Kithisak Phathavong, Mr Somdi Oudomsack), and the National University of Laos (Dr Vichith Lamxay).

J.L.-Š. would like to thank the following institutions and their staff for extensive support of her studies and fieldwork in Vietnam from 2010, and the Vietnamese authorities for granting the necessary permits: Vietnam Academy of Science and Technology (VAST), Vietnam National Museum of Nature in Hanoi (VNMN, Dr Nguyễn Quốc Bình, Dr Nguyễn Trung Minh, Prof. Lưu Đàm Cư, Dr Vũ Văn Liên), Institute of Tropical Biology in Ho Chi Minh City (ITB, Dr Lý Ngọc Sâm, Mr Trương Bá Vương, Mr Trương Quang Tâm), Prague Botanic Gardens, Czech Republic (Mr Karel Petrželka, Ms Romana Rybková) for inviting her to join their expedition in southern Vietnam. Dr Michele Rodda, Mr Aung Thame and Mr Paul Leong (all Singapore Botanic Gardens), and Mr Otakar Šída (National Museum Prague) are thanked for their help during field trips in Vietnam and Laos. Jana especially thanks her husband Michael Leong and daughter Hedi for wholeheartedly supporting her work and accompanying her on many field trips without which this book could never have been written.

We also thank the following people for their contributions to the text. Dr Vichith Lamxay and Mr Trần Hữu Đăng contributed some of the information on uses and ecology to the preliminary draft of this book, and provided us with most of the local names of gingers in

Laos and Vietnam. Dr Wolfgang Stuppy (Royal Botanic Gardens, Kew) enlightened us as to the morphology of the ginger fruit. Prof. Leonid Averyanov (Komarov Botanical Institute), Mr Maxim Nuraliev (M.V. Lomonosov Moscow State University), Dr Lý Ngọc Sâm (Institute of Tropical Biology), Mr Trần Hữu Đăng and Mathieu Leti are acknowledged for sharing their extensive collections of photographs with locality data, which significantly contributed to our knowledge of gingers in Cambodia, Laos and Vietnam. We should like to acknowledge Mr Rik Gadella, Dr David Middleton, Ms Serena Lee and Ms Bazilah Ibrahim for their support in various ways throughout the production of this book.

We thank our institutions, Singapore Botanic Gardens and Royal Botanic Garden Edinburgh for supporting our research on Zingiberaceae and providing all necessary facilities and funding.

CREDITS

The following institutions and individuals have generously contributed and granted us the permission to use the following artworks, maps and photographs.

Archives, Botanic Garden and Botanical Museum Berlin-Dahlem, Freie Universität Berlin: figure 3.3 (left, portrait of K. Schumann).

Leonid Averyanov: figures 23.1 (*Curcuma leonidii*), 25.1 (*Hedychium villosum*), 25.3 (left & right, *Hedychium villosum*), 26.5 (right, *Kaempferia rotunda*).

Cai Yi Xiong: figures 6.6 (right, little spiderhunter), 6.7 (crimson sunbird).

Chan Chew Lun: foreword chapter header (portrait of Mr Tan Jiew Hoe).

John Edmondson/Liverpool Athenaeum: figure 3.2 (right, portrait of W. Roscoe).

Rik Gadella: inner flap of back cover (view from Pha Tad Ke Botanical Garden).

Vinita Gowda: figures 6.6 (left, purple-throated Carib hummingbird), 6.8 (right, bee pollination of *Alpinia aquatica*).

W. John Kress, Ida Lopez and the Smithsonian Institution: figure 2.3 (diagrammatic representation of Zingiberales), 11.2 (portrait of W.J. Kress).

Vichith Lamxay: figures 13.1 (*Amomum tenellum*), 21.1 (*Boesenbergia laotica*), 26.1 & 26.2 (*Kaempferia fallax*), 26.7 (all, *Kaempferia laotica*), inner flap of front cover (portrait of M. Newman).

Jana Leong-Škorničková: all other images in this book.

Mathieu Leti: figures 20.1 (*Globba* sp.), 20.5 (left & right, *Globba adhaerens*).

Linnean Society of London: figure 3.2 (left, portrait of C. Linnaeus).

Lý Ngọc Sâm: figures 9.4 (left & right, *Curcuma pambrosima*), 11.4 (lower row, middle image, *Newmania orthostachys*), 12.13 (all images, *Alpinia maclurei*), 23.4 (upper right, *Curcuma pambrosima*), 23.9 (right, *Curcuma sahuynhensis*), 28 (chapter header image, *Newmania orthostachys*), 28.3 (left & right, *Newmania orthostachys*), 28.4 (left & right, *Newmania serpens*).

Mark Newman: figure 29.11 (lower right, *Zingiber nitens*).

Maxim Nuraliev: figures 12.12 (right, *Alpinia rugosa*), 15.3 (left & right, *Etlingera pavieana*), 16.2 & 16.3 (left & right, *Geostachys annamensis*), 29.10 (right, *Zingiber plicatum*).

Muséum national d'histoire naturelle, Paris: figure 3.3 (middle, portrait of F. Gagnepain).

Naturalis Biodiversity Center, The Netherlands: 3.4 (left, portrait of T. Valeton).

Nguyễn Quốc Bình: figures 12.14 (upper row, *Alpinia calcicola*), 22.3 & 22.4 (*Cautleya gracilis*), 27.1 & 27.5 (*Monolophus petelotii*).

Nguyễn Vũ Khôi: figure 28.2 (*Newmania 'cristata'*).

Peter H. Raven Library, Missouri Botanical Garden, Saint Louis, MO: figure 3.1 (cover page of Loureiro's *Flora Cochinchinensis*).

Axel Dalberg Poulsen: page 8 (*Zingiber pellitum*), figure 29.2 & 29.11 upper right (*Zingiber pellitum*).

Royal Botanic Garden Edinburgh: figures 1.3 (map from the Scottish Geographical Magazine, Volume II, 1886), 3.4 (right, portrait of R. Smith), 4.6 (diagrammatic representation of bracts, adapted from R.M. Smith 1981), 4.9 (diagrammatic flower structures, adapted from R.M. Smith 1981), 11.2 (portrait of B. L. Burtt), image of the Royal Botanic Garden Edinburgh (back cover, inner flap).

Singapore Botanic Gardens: figures 3.2 (middle, portrait of W. Roxburgh), 3.3 (right, portrait of H. N. Ridley), 3.4 (middle, portrait of R. E. Holttum), 11.1 (cover page of Schumann's Zingiberaceae in *Das Pflanzenreich*).

Otakar Šída: figures 10.3 (left, *Pommereschea lackneri*), 10.4 (*Rhynchanthus beesianus*), 22.2 (*Cautleya gracilis*).

Keooudone Souvannakhoummane: figure 21.7 (*Boesenbergia alba*), 29.1 (*Zingiber laoticum*).

Piyakaset Suksathan: figures 11.4 (upper row, middle image, *Cautleya gracilis*), 21.4 (all, *Boesenbergia burttii*), 22 (chapter header image, *Cautleya gracilis*), 22.1 (*Cautleya gracilis*), 23.8 (lower right, *Curcuma rhabdota*), inner flap of front cover (portrait of J. Leong-Škorničková).

Sandy Ross Sykes: frontispiece (painting of *Curcuma rhabdota*).

Pramote Triboun: figures 3.5 (K. & S.S. Larsen), 10.3 (right, *Pommereschea lackneri*).

University of Texas Libraries, The University of Texas at Austin: figure 1.2 (map adapted from "Indochina Atlas", published in October 1970 by the Directorate of Intelligence, Office of Basic and Geographic Intelligence, U.S. Central Intelligence Agency).

Hòn Bà Nature reserve, southern Vietnam.

Introduction

Cambodia, Laos and Vietnam are part of the Indo-Chinese continental region which includes the Andaman Islands, Burma, the Coco Islands, Cambodia, Laos, the Nicobar Islands, the Paracel Islands, the Spratly Islands, Thailand and Vietnam. The total surface area of Cambodia, Laos and Vietnam is 747,082 km².

Cambodia, Laos and Vietnam lie entirely within the tropics, stretching from 8° 25′ N in the south to 23° 22′ N in the north. Both these points are in Vietnam. The highest point of the three countries is also in Vietnam; Phan Xi Păng (Fansipan) in Lào Cai province is 3143 m high. Phou Bia is the highest point in Laos at 2819 m, while Phnum Aoral is the highest in Cambodia, 1813 m high.

The temperature in these countries normally ranges from about 20°–30° C but can go down to 5° C or slightly lower for short periods in the high mountains. The rainfall depends very much on the East Asian Monsoon which brings rain from about May to September. The rest of the year is relatively dry. Rainfall exceeds 1000 mm/year almost everywhere and can reach over 4000 mm/year in some mountainous areas. The driest part is SE Vietnam with an average annual rainfall of around 650 mm at Phan Rang.

As expected in tropical countries with abundant rainfall, the natural vegetation is forest of various kinds, except in certain habitats, such as beaches and high mountain tops. Tropical rain forest, as found near

Fig. 1.1 Montane forest in Bạch Mã National Park, Vietnam.

the equator is uncommon because of the strong dry season. The lowland forests of Cambodia, Laos and Vietnam are evergreen where the dry season is short and deciduous where it is longer. One common forest type in Cambodia and Laos has been called Dry Dipterocarp Forest by Asian ecologists. Ecologically, it corresponds to savanna in Africa and the Neotropics. A very special type of forest occurs in central Cambodia; this is flooded forest which is dry for part of the year and flooded in the rainy season. At higher altitudes, montane forests take over. These are characterised by species in the tree families Fagaceae and Lauraceae. There are small areas of natural grassland, and very important limestone areas with many unique species growing in them. Limestone is particularly common in Laos and Vietnam.

Gingers may be found in most habitat types in Cambodia, Laos and Vietnam. They are never aquatic and rarely epiphytic but mostly grow on the ground in forest of one kind or another. Many are geophytes, that is, they produce their leaves and flowers in the rainy season and then die back to the underground rhizome for the dry season.

WHERE IS INDO-CHINA?

The term Indo-China has a confusing array of meanings. One is very similar to the phytogeographical unit called the Indo-Chinese continental region above. In some publications the related term Indo-Chinese Peninsula (*presqu'île indochinoise* in French) is found. This again is roughly equivalent to the Indo-Chinese continental region of tropical Asia.

In another sense, Indo-China is restricted to the former French colonies of Cambodia, Laos and Vietnam, an area much smaller than the Indo-Chinese continental region. During the French colonial period, Vietnam was composed of three main regions which were colonised at different times. Annam was the central part of Vietnam with its historical capital at Hue, Cochinchina lay to its south with Saigon as its capital and Tonkin was to its north with Hanoi as its capital. These names are no longer current but commonly seen in older writings and on the labels of dried plant collections.

THE GINGERS OF CAMBODIA, LAOS & VIETNAM

The greatest concentration of genera of gingers is found in the Indo-Chinese continental region. By contrast, the greatest concentration of species occurs in

Fig. 1.2 Map of Cambodia, Laos and Vietnam. Adapted from "Indochina Atlas", published in October 1970 by the Directorate of Intelligence, Office of Basic and Geographic Intelligence, U.S. Central Intelligence Agency.

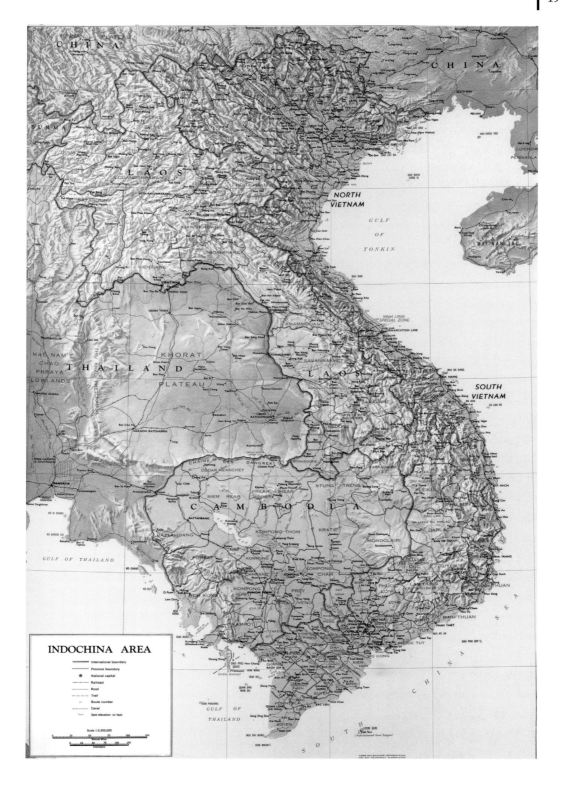

INTRODUCTION

the islands of Southeast Asia, Indonesia, Malaysia (Sarawak and Sabah), Brunei, the Philippines, Timor Leste and Papua New Guinea. Revisions of the gingers have only been completed in Peninsular Malaysia, Singapore and Borneo yet, even here, significant new discoveries, such as new genera and new species, have been made since these publications came out and are still being made. In the rest of SE Asia, new species and genera are being found at a great rate but the forests are also disappearing very fast so there is a race on to describe and document all the species before they go extinct so that they can be conserved for the future.

The most recent account of the gingers of Cambodia, Laos and Vietnam is to be found in volume 6 of the *Flore générale de l'Indochine*, which is more than a century old.

HISTORY OF BOTANY IN CAMBODIA, LAOS & VIETNAM

The earliest botanical publication to treat Cambodia, Laos and Vietnam was Loureiro's *Flora cochinchinensis*, published at Lisbon in 1790. At that time the term Cochinchina meant something close to the whole Indo-Chinese continental region. Loureiro himself lived at Hue so most of the plants he treated came from central Annam, to which he added species from China, India and the east coast of Africa.

It was about a hundred years until the next significant publications. By a decree of June 1877, the Governor of the Colony put Jean Baptiste Louis Pierre, the Director of Saigon Botanic Garden, in charge of the *Flore forestière de la Cochinchine* (1880–1907) and the *Flore générale de l'Indochine*. The former, as the name suggests, treated trees of Cochinchina which by this time meant only southern Vietnam. The *Flore forestière* was never completed and, at Pierre's death in 1905, none of the *Flore générale de l'Indochine* had been published.

The responsibility for the *Flore générale de l'Indochine* then passed to the Muséum national d'histoire naturelle in Paris where François Gagnepain and Achille Eugène Finet were the editors for a short time until H. Lecomte was made professor at the museum. Lecomte became director of the *Flore* and Gagnepain became editorial secretary.

At the outset, the *Flore générale de l'Indochine* covered all the Indo-Chinese Peninsula except Burma and Peninsular Malaysia (Gagnepain, 1944). That's to say, it covered Thailand, as well as Cambodia, Laos and Vietnam. Revisions were based almost entirely on collections held at the herbarium in Paris with little reference to other material.

Fig. 1.3 | Map of Indo-China showing proposed Burma-Siam-China Railway, from the Scottish Geographical Magazine, Volume II, 1886.

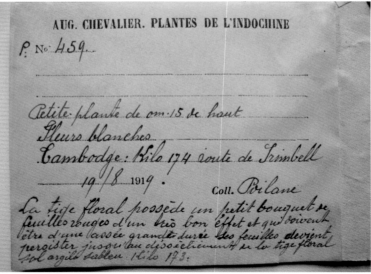

Fig. 1.4 Specimen and detail of the label of *Curcuma sparganiifolia* collected by Eugène Poilane in June 1875 in Cambodia.

French botanists amassed significant collections during the late 19ᵗʰ and early 20ᵗʰ centuries. The most numerous collections were made by Auguste Chevalier and Eugène Poilane who gathered more than 10,000 specimens each. Six more collectors, including Louis Pierre and Clovis Thorel collected more than 5,000 specimens while another eight collected more than 1,000. More detail about the flora and collectors in Cambodia, Laos and Vietnam may be found in the "Tome préliminaire" to the *Flore générale de l'Indochine* which came out in 1944.

Country	No. of collections per 100 km²
Cambodia	4
Laos	3
Vietnam	14
Thailand	50
United Kingdom	1700

Table 1. Collection density of herbarium specimens (D.J. Middleton 2003 & pers. comm.)

Historical events all but prevented botanical work in Cambodia, Laos and Vietnam between the Second World War and the 1990s though some collections were made during interludes of peace in the 1950s and early 1960s. Taking all known collections together, it is possible to calculate the "collecting density" in each country which is the number of collections per 100 km². These figures are compared to neighbouring countries and to the United Kingdom in Table 1, showing that *Cambodia, Laos* and *Vietnam* are still desperately undercollected.

Gingers & their relatives

Gingers are plants in the family Zingiberaceae which include ginger, turmeric, cardamom and about 1500 wild species. Interest in these plants among botanists and horticulturists has grown rapidly in recent decades and illustrated guide books to the species of Peninsular Malaysia and Singapore, Thailand, and Borneo have been published, showing the rich diversity and beauty to be found in the family.

The scientific name of the ginger used in cookery and medicine is *Zingiber officinale*, turmeric is *Curcuma longa* and cardamom is *Elettaria cardamomum*. Each of these species belongs in a different genus but they are only three of the 53 or so genera in the family.

One genus, *Renealmia*, is found in the tropics of America and Africa. Three more, *Aframomum*, *Aulotandra* and *Siphonochilus*, only occur in Africa and Madagascar. The others, nearly 50 genera and most of the species, are found in the forests of tropical and subtropical Asia from Sri Lanka and India to Vanuatu and Fiji in the western Pacific, taking in southern China and southern Japan to the north and Australia, as far south as northern New South Wales.

The ginger family shares a number of characters with seven other families which together make an order, called the Zingiberales. These eight families are highly evolved monocotyledons which have been recognised as a natural group since the time of Linnaeus or before, though the classification of the genera into families has changed. Linnaeus, in his *Species plantarum* of 1753, placed *Canna*, *Amomum*, *Costus*, *Alpinia*, *Maranta*, *Curcuma* and *Kaempferia*, which are now in the order Zingiberales, in his class *Monandria monogynia*, flowers with one female part

Fig. 2.1 | Cardamom (*Elettaria cardamomum*).

Fig. 2.2 | Ginger (*Zingiber officinale*, left) and turmeric (*Curcuma longa*, right).

and one male part, along with some other genera which are no longer considered to be closely related to the Zingiberales. When he published the tenth edition of his *Systema Naturae* in 1758, Linnaeus placed these genera in a group called Scitamineae, from the Latin *scitamenta*, meaning delicacies. Nowadays, it would not be correct to use this name in scientific writings but it is still seen in publications from the 18th to the early 20th century.

Members of the ginger order are easily recognised in the field as there are few other large, monocotyledonous herbs which can be mistaken for them. A few species of grass (Gramineae) and sedge (Cyperaceae) look like Zingiberales at first glance but their small, chaffy flowers are quite different. Young rattan plants (Palmae) can also resemble Zingiberales when seen at a distance but they are always more lignified, with compound leaves and spines on the stems. No spines are found in Zingiberales and the leaves are always simple. Some members of Araceae can also resemble gingers but close examination of the leaves, which have no ligules and often have a leathery lamina with palmate venation, will distinguish them.

Fig. 2.3 | Diagrammatic representation of the relationships of the families of Zingiberales.

The Zingiberales are essentially tropical plants though some extend into subtropical and warm temperate latitudes to 37° N (*Canna flaccida* in Virginia, USA) and to 34° 30' S (*Strelitzia* in the eastern Cape, South Africa). They occupy a wide altitudinal range, from sea level to >5,000 m alt. Certain species of *Roscoea* in the Himalaya and *Riedelia* in New Guinea reach the highest altitudes.

Most Zingiberales are understorey herbs of forests though many bananas (Musaceae) are adapted to colonisation of clearings caused by falling trees, storm damage or landslips where the forest canopy is opened. *Aframomum* (Zingiberaceae) forms extensive colonies in gaps in African rain forest and is an important food source for herbivorous mammals such as elephant and gorilla. Some Zingiberales have adapted to living in monsoon forest with a strong dry season by becoming deciduous. They survive the dry season as underground rhizomes which sprout at the beginning of the rainy season. These plants are called geophytes.

Most Zingiberales are perennial plants which flower every year, once they are mature. In the species which bear their inflorescences at the tops of the leafy shoots, the shoot dies after flowering and fruiting. There are a few exceptions to this rule in the Marantaceae and Strelitziaceae. *Ensete* (Musaceae) is unusual in that the plants do not produce suckers from the rhizomes and individuals die completely after flowering and fruiting, leaving the next generation to grow from seed.

The flowers of Zingiberales are complex in their structure, almost always zygomorphic, leading us to suppose that they are pollinated by a small number of sophisticated pollinators. Research shows, however, that the pollinators are very diverse. The flowers of many Musaceae, some *Heliconia* and *Phenakospermum* open at night and are pollinated by bats. Few Zingiberaceae species flower at night and these are pollinated by moths. Bee pollination has been observed in Costaceae, Marantaceae and Zingiberaceae while birds are adapted to the larger and tougher flowers of some Costaceae, Heliconiaceae, Marantaceae, Zingiberaceae and *Strelitzia*. Finally the remarkable relationship between *Ravenala madagascariensis* and ruffed lemurs, both endemic to Madagascar, should be noted, and dung-beetle pollination of the malodorous flowers of Bornean *Orchidantha*.

Seed dispersal is almost always by means of animals and rarely by water. The seeds of most Zingiberales have a fleshy outgrowth from the base of the seed called an aril. It may be small, restricted to near the base of the seed or large, covering the seed entirely. It is rich in oils and proteins, making it an attractive source of food. Ants are known to carry away the seeds of some Marantaceae and Zingiberaceae. Birds are also known to be attracted to some ginger species with brightly coloured arils, such as *Hedychium*. Rodents and other mammals disperse larger seeds and those with sweet and sour arils, such as those of Musaceae and some Zingiberaceae.

Vegetative reproduction is important in the life cycle of many species. The most common method is persistence of the rhizome which can branch, allowing an individual to colonise suitable habitat. In some cases, vegetative propagules, such as bulbils and plantlets, are also produced. These enable a plant to disperse over a wider area than it could simply by extension of the rhizome. The reproductive biology of the Zingiberaceae is discussed in more detail in chapter 6.

The order Zingiberales consists of eight plant families, which are now briefly introduced.

BANANA FAMILY (Musaceae)

The Banana family comprises three genera, *Ensete* and *Musa,* and *Musella*, and c. 40 spp., distributed widely in the Old World tropics. Bananas and plantains are widely cultivated throughout the tropics as a source of fruit, starch, fibre and as ornamentals. They are large herbs with spirally arranged leaves without ligules. The inflorescence always appears at the top of the leafy shoot and the flowers are functionally unisexual with females at the base and males at the apex of the inflorescence. There are usually 5 stamens in male flowers, rarely 6, the "missing" stamen being seen as a staminode. The fruit is a berry with seeds embedded in a fleshy pulp.

Fifteen species are native to Cambodia, Laos and Vietnam, two of *Ensete*, 12 species and one variety of *Musa* and one species of *Musella*.

Fig. 2.4 Fruits and seeds of *Ensete glaucum* are prized in Vietnam for their medicinal properties.

Fig. 2.5 | *Musa haekkinenii*, a new and highly ornamental species, was described from northern Vietnam in 2013.

ORCHIDANTHA FAMILY (Lowiaceae)

The Lowiaceae consists of a single genus, *Orchidantha*, with about 20 species distributed in China, Thailand, Laos, Vietnam, Peninsular Malaysia and Borneo. No uses have been reported but some species are growing in popularity as ornamentals for their tufted foliage.

Orchidanthas are small to large forest herbs with distichously arranged leaves which lack ligules. The inflorescences arise near the ground on a leafless peduncle which is often at least partly subterranean and made up of repeating units without specialised subtending bracts. The flowers are bisexual and bilaterally symmetrical (zygomorphic), often large, with 5 fertile stamens. The labellum often emits a strong smell of rotten meat, fungus or dung. The ovary is linked to the base of the style by a long, neck-like extension and the fruit is a trilocular capsule opening by three valves, each locule containing several seeds with hair-like arils.

Only three species are known to occur in Vietnam and one species in Laos. There are no reports of Lowiaceae from Cambodia yet.

Fig. 2.6 | *Orchidantha laotica* (left) and *Orchidantha vietnamica* (right) were originally described from herbarium material. Recent collections have helped to clarify their identities.

Fig. 2.7 | *Orchidantha virosa* is the most robust of the four species known from Laos and Vietnam.

BIRD-OF-PARADISE FAMILY (Strelitziaceae)

Three genera are classified in the Strelitziaceae, two of them consisting of a single species (monotypic). *Ravenala madagascariensis*, widely cultivated in the tropics and known as Traveller's Palm, is endemic to Madagascar. Similar in its large size and habit is *Phenakospermum guyannense* which is native to tropical South America. *Strelitzia*, with 4–5 species, is native to southern Africa, and several species are cultivated in the tropics and beyond as garden plants and for cut flowers. Most Strelitziaceae are robust plants, often with woody stems. The leaves are arranged distichously and have no ligule. The inflorescences, which have rigid bracts that subtend a few flowers each, appear either terminally or laterally. The flowers are bisexual and bilaterally symmetrical (zygomorphic), fragrant or odourless, with 5 or 6 (*Ravenala* only) functional stamens. There are many ovules in each locule and the fruit is a woody, trilocular capsule splitting at maturity, exposing seeds with a well-developed, brightly coloured, orange, red or electric blue aril.

Only *Ravenala madagascariensis* and *Strelitzia reginae* are seen in Cambodia, Laos and Vietnam.

Fig. 2.8 | *Ravenala madagascariensis,* a common sight in tropical cities, is often mistaken for a palm.

Fig. 2.9 | *Strelitzia reginae* is the most commonly cultivated species for the cut flower industry.

HELICONIA FAMILY (Heliconiaceae)

A single genus, *Heliconia*, with more than 220 species, makes up the family. Most species are native in tropical America, with some six species in the Old World tropics, from the Moluccas to the western Pacific. Many *Heliconia* species are cultivated as ornamentals throughout the tropics.

Heliconias are medium-sized to large plants with distichous leaves lacking ligules. The inflorescences, which appear at the top of the leafy shoots in most species, rarely on a separate peduncle, consist of a few to many, well-developed and usually brightly coloured bracts, each enclosing a cluster of flowers. The flowers are bisexual and bilaterally symmetrical (zygomorphic), with 5 fertile stamens and a solitary ovule in each locule. The fruit is a drupe, ripening blue in New World species and orange to red in Old World species. The seeds lack an aril.

A few, common species of *Heliconia* have been introduced into cultivation in Cambodia, Laos and Vietnam.

Fig. 2.10 *Heliconia psittacorum* (upper left) and *Heliconia rostrata* (upper right) are commonly cultivated *Heliconia* species. *Heliconia solomonensis* (below) is an example of an Old World species.

SPIRAL GINGER FAMILY (Costaceae)

Seven genera and about 150 species are currently recognised in the Spiral Ginger family. The largest genus, *Costus* (c. 110 spp.), is confined to tropical America and tropical Africa. Three more small genera are confined to the Neotropics, namely *Chamaecostus* (8 species), *Monocostus* (1 species) and *Dimerocostus* (2 species). *Cheilocostus*, with at least 5 species, is native in tropical Asia, reaching as far east as New Guinea while *Paracostus* with only 2 species occurs in West Africa & Borneo. *Tapeinocheilos*, with about 16 species, is found from the Moluccas to NE Australia and the Solomon Islands. Many species are cultivated throughout the tropics as ornamentals. The widespread *Cheilocostus speciosus* is used locally in medicine and as a source of starch.

Spiral Gingers are small to large herbs with spirally arranged, ligulate leaves. The inflorescences appear either at the top of the leafy shoots or on separate leafless shoots. The flowers are bisexual and bilaterally symmetrical (zygomorphic), with one fertile stamen. The style is clasped between the two anther thecae and the stigma is held just above the anther. The labellum is formed of 5 connate staminodes and usually wraps round the back of the anther making a trumpet-shaped flower. The fruit is usually a trilocular capsule, containing numerous small seeds with white or yellow aril.

At least three species of *Cheilocostus* are native to Cambodia, Laos and Vietnam.

Fig. 2.11 Various wild and cultivated morphological forms of *Cheilocostus speciosus*, known in cultivation as the crepe ginger, occur in Cambodia, Laos and Vietnam.

Fig. 2.12 Described as *Costus tonkinensis* and awaiting formal transfer to *Cheilocostus*, this species is common in northern parts of Laos and Vietnam, and southern China.

Fig. 2.13 African *Costus tappenbeckianus* (left) can produce flowers near the ground as well as on the tops of leafy shoots. *Costus woodsonii* (right) is an example of a bird-pollinated, neotropical *Costus*.

GINGER FAMILY (Zingiberaceae)

The ginger family consists of about 53 genera and more than 1500 species and is pantropical with its centre of distribution in the Indo-Malayan region. Several species are of great economic importance as spices, medicinal plants, ornamentals, dyes and vegetables, and many more have minor uses.

Gingers are small to large herbs with ethereal oils in their rhizomes and leafy shoots, and distichous, ligulate leaves. The inflorescences appear either at the top of the leafy shoots or on separate leafless shoots and the flowers are bisexual and bilaterally symmetrical (zygomorphic), odourless or rarely fragrant, with one fertile stamen. Rarely, in certain species not native in Cambodia, Laos and Vietnam, flowers with functionally male and functionally female flowers occur on the same plant. The style

Fig. 2.14 | *Alpinia monopleura*, a native of Sulawesi, Indonesia, is one of the very few species in which separate male and female flowers occur in a single inflorescence.

is clasped between the two pollen sacs of the anther and the stigma is held just above it. The labellum is composed of 2 connate staminodes and is very variable in shape and size. Two other staminodes are present, called lateral staminodes, either as petaloid organs or small swellings or needle-shaped organs at the base of the labellum, or completely suppressed and invisible. The fruit is a unilocular or trilocular capsule, dehiscing irregularly by valves, or one of several kinds of indehiscent fruit, such as a hesperidium. The seeds are arillate, the aril being white, pale yellow or red, sometimes markedly sweet or sour.

Given the sharp rise in the number of species reported from Cambodia, Laos and Vietnam in recent years, we estimate that the total may exceed 300.

Fig. 2.15 | *Renealmia* (*R. polypus*, left), with about 75 species, is the only genus of Zingiberaceae in the Neotropics. *Burbidgea* (*B. schizocheila*, right) is a small genus of mostly epiphytic plants endemic to Borneo.

Fig. 2.16 *Aframomum chrysanthum* is one of approximately 80 species of this large African genus. The fruits and seeds of a number of species of *Aframomum* are used in the same way as cardamom.

CANNA FAMILY (Cannaceae)

The family consists of a single genus, *Canna*, with 10 species native in tropical and subtropical America, and many cultivars and hybrids. Both the wild species and many cultivars are planted, mainly in the tropics and subtropics, as ornamentals and for starch production.

Cannas are medium-sized to large herbs with distichously to spirally arranged leaves which have no ligule. The inflorescences appear at the top of the leafy shoots and the flowers are bisexual, asymmetrical and consist of 3 sepals, 3 petals and 1–4(–5) staminodes. The single stamen has only one functional pollen sac. There are many ovules in the three locules of the ovary. The fruit is a loculicidal, trilocular dry capsule. The seeds are round and very hard, lacking an aril.

Canna indica is often cultivated in Vietnam for its starchy tubers, the starch being processed into noodles. *Canna* hybrids are grown as ornamentals throughout Cambodia, Laos and Vietnam, especially in the cities.

Fig. 2.17 | *Canna indica* (left) is commonly cultivated while various hybrids of *Canna × generalis* (right) are splendid ornamentals.

PRAYER PLANT FAMILY (Marantaceae)

A pantropical family of 31 genera and more than 550 species strongly centred in the Neotropics. *Maranta arundinacea* is cultivated on a large scale for its high-quality starch and several species, mainly of *Calathea*, are cultivated throughout the tropics as ornamentals.

Prayer plants are small to large, often branched herbs. The leaves are arranged distichously and there is a swollen (pulvinate) petiole near the point of attachment to the leaf blade. The inflorescence may be terminal or lateral and the flowers are bisexual, asymmetrical, and borne in mirror-image pairs. The sepals are distinct and there is a floral tube composed of one hooded staminode, one fleshy staminode, 1 or 2 petaloid staminodes and the single stamen with only one functional theca, intriguingly arranged in an explosive mechanism to aid pollination. Each of the 1 or 3 locules of the ovary has a single ovule. The fruit is often a loculicidal capsule but may be indehiscent, berry-like or caryopsis-like. The seeds are usually arillate.

Fewer than 15 species are native in Cambodia, Laos and Vietnam.

Fig. 2.18 | *Phrynium tonkinensis* (left) grows in montane forests in northern Vietnam. *Stachyphrynium spicatum* (right) is a lowland species which can be seen in all three countries.

Fig. 2.19 | Leaves of *Phrynium placentarium,* which can be seen in the wild as well as cultivated, are widely used in Vietnam for wrapping sticky rice cakes.

Fig. 2.20 | Freshly boiled starchy rhizomes of arrowroot (*Maranta arundinacea*) sold in Vietnam are an enjoyable street snack.

Fig. 2.21 | *Schumannianthus dichotomus* is widespread throughout SE Asia including Cambodia, Laos and Vietnam.

Taxonomic history

Zingiberaceae have been known to medical practitioners throughout written history, being first mentioned in Vedic texts. The name itself comes from an Indian word, perhaps Malayalam ഇഞ്ചി (inchi) or Tamil இஞ்சி (inji) which was taken into Sanskrit as singabera and Latin as zingiber.

The first descriptions of these plants in botanical science are those by **Carl Linnaeus**, who placed them in a class called *Monandria monogynia* in his *Species plantarum* of 1753.

In the 1770s, the Danish botanist **Johan Gerhard Koenig** travelled in Asia and visited parts of peninsular Thailand, in particular Junk Ceylon, now known as Phuket. He made a number of herbarium collections of Zingiberaceae and his unfinished descriptions were published, without his permission, by Retzius in 1783. For a long time, it was believed that all Koenig's collections had been lost but some have recently been found at the Naturhistorisk Museum, Copenhagen. Among these are specimens of *Amomum uliginosum* J. Koenig and *Etlingera elatior* Giseke.

The oldest surviving specimens of Zingiberaceae from the area of Cambodia, Laos and Vietnam are probably those of Loureiro. **João de Loureiro** was a Portuguese Jesuit missionary and botanist who, in 1742, travelled to Cochinchina (now southern Vietnam), where he remained for 35 years, living chiefly at Hue. He published the first flora of Southeast Asia, the *Flora Cochinchinensis* in 1790 in which 13 species in three genera of Zingiberaceae are described.

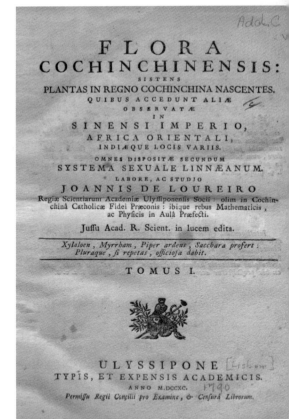

Fig. 3.1 | Cover page of Loureiro's *Flora Cochinchinensis*.

Fig. 3.4 | Théodoric Valeton (left); Richard Eric Holttum (middle); Rosemary Smith (right).

Richard Eric Holttum was based in Singapore Botanic Gardens so he was also able to study living plants.

Brian Lawrence Burtt, a botanist at the Royal Botanic Garden, Edinburgh began to collect Zingiberaceae while exploring Sarawak for Gesneriaceae in the 1960s. He and his colleague, **Rosemary Smith**, produced a series of papers in the late 1960s and 1970s, after which Smith continued alone, publishing a number of significant contributions, such as *A review of Bornean Zingiberaceae* from 1985–1989, and a new classification of *Alpinia* in 1990.

Kai Larsen visited Thailand in the 1950s and maintained close links with the country for the rest of his life. His first papers on the Zingiberaceae were published in the early 1960s and he continued to work on them from then on. Kai Larsen's Thai publications are of great significance in Cambodia, Laos and Vietnam since Thailand belongs in the same floristic region as they do.

Fig. 3.5 | Kai Larsen and his wife Supee Saksuwan Larsen have dedicated their lives to the Thai flora.

The ginger plant

Gingers are perennial rhizomatous herbs. Most grow on the ground but a few species grow on trees or in pockets of humus on rocks. Some grow solitarily, or form dense or loose clumps, while others may appear to be solitary stems but are connected underground by creeping rhizomes. Many are around 1–2 m tall but the smallest, for example some *Curcuma* and *Kaempferia* species, are just a few centimetres tall, while some species of *Apinia* and *Etlingera* in Cambodia, Laos and Vietnam may reach 4 metres in height. The leafy shoots of the majority of species in subfamily Zingiberoideae die back during the dry season, while those in subfamily Alpinioideae are evergreen.

RHIZOME

The rhizome is a much-condensed stem which can be simple or variously branched. The branches may be short and stout or slender and creeping; all are capable of initiating new shoots. Most rhizomes are embedded in the soil or at least partially covered at ground level but those of some species of *Etlingera*, *Hornstedtia*, *Amomum* and *Geostachys* are held above the ground by stilt roots. The size and shape of the branches, and the rhizome architecture are helpful for identification in several genera, such as *Curcuma* and *Zingiber*. The rhizomes are usually light brown in colour externally but, internally, they can be white, cream, light to sulphur-yellow with bluish or green shades, pink, orange, grey, blue, or greenish blue to dark violet-brown. While the internal colour can be quite specific to some species, it can vary

Fig. 4.1 | Root tubers of *Kaempferia rotunda*.

Fig. 4.2 | Internal colours of rhizomes (from left): *Curcuma phaeocaulis, Kaempferia galanga, Hedychium* sp., *Curcuma zanthorrhiza* (note the orange colour of the root tubers).

considerably in others. The scent and taste of the rhizomes can be very helpful but these characters are even more subjective than colours making them difficult to describe and assess.

The roots of many deciduous species, mainly those of genera in the Zingiberoideae, expand along their entire length (e.g. *Globba*) or at one point (e.g. *Curcuma, Kaempferia*) and contain a lot of starch. They are called root tubers and they sustain the plant through the dry period, when the leafy shoot dies back. Root tubers cannot sprout. They are light brown externally, usually white to cream coloured, yellowish or, rarely, orange internally. They are located either near or right next to the rhizome or its branches, or at up to 50 cm from the rhizome. There is usually only one tuber per root, commonly located at its end but, sometimes, there can be a series of tubers on a root, looking like a string of beads.

LEAFY SHOOTS

As explained above, the true stem of gingers, called the rhizome, is a much-condensed stem. The stem-like part of the plant is called a false stem or pseudostem. A typical ginger leaf consists of a leaf sheath at the base, a ligule, a petiole (which may be well-developed or missing) and the leaf blade (also called lamina). The pseudostem is made of tightly clasping leaf sheaths and the leaf blades are each borne at 180° to the last, an arrangement called distichous. The plane of distichy may be parallel to the direction of growth of the rhizome, which is usually the case in the Zingiberoideae,

Fig. 4.3 Habit types (from left): clearly distichous (*Amomum* sp.), tufted (*Curcuma* sp.), *Kaempferia* with pseudostem buried and leaves appressed to the ground.

or transverse to it, which occurs in the Alpinioideae. In many species the false stem is well-developed, with numerous leaf blades distichously arranged. In others, the leaf sheaths clasp each other loosely so that the distichous arrangement is difficult to see. When a number of these loose pseudostems grow together, the plant may look like a tuft. In some cases the false stem may be partly or fully buried in the ground (e.g. *Kaempferia*) or appears to be missing, but it is almost always visible at the beginning of the season and deteriorates as the central inflorescence protrudes from the middle of the leaves.

The leaf sheaths are usually open to the base but, in a few genera, they are partly or fully tubular (e.g. *Cautleya*, *Newmania*, *Roscoea*, some *Zingiber* spp.). The colour of the leaf sheaths and presence of strong reticulation or a covering of silver hairs may be useful for identification in some genera (e.g. *Etlingera*, *Hornstedtia*).

A ligule is present at the junction of the petiole and sheath or the junction of the blade and sheath, when the petiole is reduced. The ligule may be small and inconspicuous or large, to 5 cm long, of various textures and shapes. Very rarely, the ligule may be tubular (e.g. *Zingiber neotruncatum*) or completely missing.

The petiole may be more or less developed or reduced, in which case the leaf blades are said to be sessile. In *Zingiber*, the petiole is swollen at the base and is called a pulvinus.

THE GINGER PLANT

Fig. 4.4 Ligules (from left): reticulate leaf sheaths and red ligule of *Amomum chinense*, tough and hairy ligule of *Alpinia blepharocalyx*, thin membranaceous ligule of *Zingiber orbiculatum*, tubular ligule and pulvinus of *Zingiber neotruncatum*.

The shape of the leaf blade varies greatly in the ginger family. Most commonly it is ovate, elliptic or weakly obovate, but it may be linear in certain species (e.g. *Kaempferia fallax*) and, in others, nearly round (e.g. *Kaempferia marginata*). The shape of the base and apex can be helpful for identification in certain genera. The venation is parallel in all gingers but, in some species, certain veins are more prominent than others, resulting in a neatly plicate surface. The upper surface of the lamina may vary from light to deep green above, or may be ornamented with silver and bronze patterns (*Kaempferia*, *Zingiber*), have a purple or violet patch along the midrib (*Curcuma*) or red blotches (*Etlingera*). The lower surface of the lamina is usually paler green or flushed to a certain degree with red, sometimes even being a solid, deep wine-red colour. Both sides of the leaf blade or part of it, such as the midrib or margin, may be glabrous or variously hairy. The hairs may be short and rough or long and silky, sparse or so dense that the surface appears to be woolly, velvety or silvery. While the presence and pattern of the indumentum may be constant and helpful for determining some species, they are also known to be highly variable in some seed-setting species and often vary even within a population.

INFLORESCENCE

The inflorescence of gingers is always terminal and has few to many flowers. It can be much branched and lax in some *Alpinia* species, with reduced pedicels, forming a spike in *Zingiber* or with a congested rachis, forming a globose inflorescence resembling a head in *Etlingera*. It arises either on a vegetative leafy shoot and is then

Fig. 4.5 Inflorescences (from left): central inflorescence of *Alpinia oxymitra*, lateral inflorescence of *Zingiber orbiculatum*, lateral inflorescence of *Kaempferia rotunda* appears before the leaves; central inflorescence breaking through the pseudostem in *Zingiber monophyllum*.

called a central inflorescence, or on a separate leafless shoot, which is usually much shorter than the leafy shoot and is called a lateral (or radical) inflorescence. Certain species of *Curcuma*, *Globba* and *Zingiber* are capable of producing inflorescences in both positions, even on the same plant. While most gingers flower when their leafy shoot is at least partly developed, a lateral inflorescence appears before the leaves develop in some species of *Curcuma*, *Gagnepainia* and *Kaempferia*. When a species with a poorly developed pseudostem produces a central inflorescence with a short peduncle at ground level, it may appear to be lateral. Finally, a central inflorescence may break sideways through the pseudostem in *Alpinia*, *Curcuma*, and *Zingiber*. The inflorescence of all Zingiberaceae is, in principle, a thyrse, composed of cymose partial inflorescences called cincinni. The flowers in each cincinnus usually open in sequence, one at a time. The direction of flowering is from base to top in the great majority of genera but *Boesenbergia* is characterised by top to base flowering. The approximate number of flowers per cincinnus is useful as an additional character but, in many species, it may vary even within an inflorescence, usually with more flowers per cincinnus at the base of the inflorescence. Cincinni are often subtended by persistent fertile bracts which are spirally arranged in most genera but may also be distichous or secund, as in *Distichochlamys* and *Monolophus*. While the bracts are free to the base in nearly all genera, they are connate to each other and form pouches in most *Curcuma* species. Some genera, such as *Etlingera*, also have sterile involucral bracts surrounding the base of the inflorescence while, in some *Curcuma* species, there are sterile and often much enlarged and brightly coloured bracts at

the top of the inflorescence which are called a coma. Sometimes the fertile bracts are caducous, falling from the inflorescence soon after the first flower buds open; this is found in some *Alpinia* and *Siliquamomum* species.

In most genera, each flower in a cincinnus is enfolded by one or more bracteoles which may be tubular or open to the base, well developed, reduced or, in some genera and species, completely missing.

Fig. 4.6 | Diagrammatic representation of a bract subtending a single flower (left) and a bract subtending a cincinnus of three flowers (right). Bract (dark green), bracteole (light green) flower (orange).

FLOWER

Most ginger flowers last only a couple of hours to a day but may last up to three days, mostly in species that grow at high altitudes. A few species, such as *Kaempferia fallax*, flower at night, a phenomenon known as nocturnal anthesis. Gingers have highly specialised bilaterally symmetrical (zygomorphic) and bisexual flowers. While the calyx (sepals) and corolla lobes (petals) are usually relatively inconspicuous, the pollinators are attracted by elaborate petal-like structures called lateral staminodes and labellum. These have evolved from four of the six stamens that are fertile in a typical monocotyledonous flower, such as a lily. Two anthers of the outer whorl have been transformed into lateral staminodes; two anthers of the inner whorl have developed into a labellum. Only one anther of the inner whorl is functional and the frontal (anterior) stamen of the outer whorl is altogether suppressed.

Each flower consists of calyx, floral tube, staminal tube (not always present), corolla lobes, lateral staminodes, labellum, stamen, epigynous glands, style, stigma and ovary. While the basic number and arrangement of floral parts are quite uniform throughout the family, there is great variation in the size and shape of the parts, especially in the labellum and lateral staminodes.

The calyx is usually thin and tubular, with one to three teeth and split down one side in most species.

Fig. 4.7 Arrangement of bracts (from left): spirally arranged bracts with sterile coma bracts (*Curcuma aeruginosa*), distichous (*Distichochlamys* sp.), secund (*Monolophus bracteatus*).

The floral tube (often incorrectly called the corolla tube) is the tubular part of the ginger flower which is formed by fusion of the bases of the staminodial and corolla whorls, until they eventually separate from each other, diverging into staminodes, labellum, anther and corolla lobes. In most gingers the corolla lobes diverge from the apex of the floral tube at the same level as the labellum, lateral staminodes and filament but, in a number of genera, such as *Etlingera*, *Globba* and some species of *Curcuma*, the corolla lobes diverge from the floral tube first, while the inner part of the floral tube, made up of the bases of the staminodes and filament, is prolonged beyond it, forming a staminodial tube (or androecial tube) before it divides into the labellum, lateral staminodes and filament. The internal structure of the floral tube varies among the genera. For example, in *Curcuma*, the tube is densely hairy at the point where the funnel-shaped part of the tube starts and often there is a ring of swollen tissues with a groove for supporting the style. The hairy ring appears to serve as a barrier to protect the nectar reward from nectar robbers. It also helps mechanically to increase the chance of passing the pollen onto the back of the pollinators, as they have to probe deeply and struggle to reach the nectar reward. In other genera, there is a groove guiding and protecting the style along all or part of the dorsal side of the floral tube.

As explained above, the outer layer of the floral tube separates into three corolla lobes at a certain point. The dorsal corolla lobe stands behind the anther and is usually

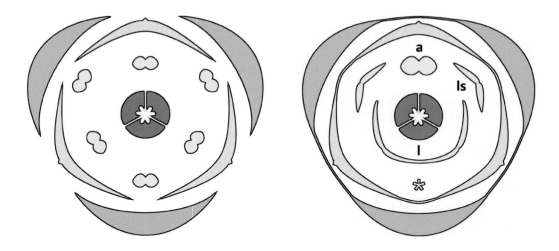

Fig. 4.8 | Diagrammatic representation of a typical monocot flower (left) and a ginger flower (right): green—sepals, in gingers forming a tubular calyx, orange—petals, in gingers represented by outer layer of floral tube and corolla lobes, yellow—anthers, in gingers only one is fully functional (a), one is reduced (asterisk), two are transformed into lateral staminodes (ls) and two are transformed and merged into the labellum (l), the bases of stamen and staminodes fuse to form the inner layer of the floral tube.

slightly larger than the laterals. It is often hooded and usually embraces at least the base of the lateral staminodes, if these are well developed. The two lateral corolla lobes are often appressed to the labellum below. In some genera (e.g. *Gagnepainia*, some species of *Distichochlamys*) the corolla lobes are strongly reflexed and roll up shortly after the flower bud opens or they may be nearly linear and droop, as in many *Hedychium* species.

The labellum and lateral staminodes are prominent features of the ginger flower. The lateral staminodes are placed at each side of the base of the labellum and may be joined to the labellum (e.g. *Zingiber* or *Siliquamomum*). They can be conspicuous and petal-like (most Zingiberoideae), reduced to small tooth-like structures, or even completely lacking. The labellum is the showiest part of the ginger flower and comes in a wide range of shapes and colours. It may be oval, obscurely or prominently bilobed or trilobed and usually more or less emarginate. The central part of the labellum is usually thicker, sometimes forming grooves (some *Curcuma* spp.) or elaborate structures (*Gagnepainia*) and often differs in colour, probably to serve as a guide for pollinators.

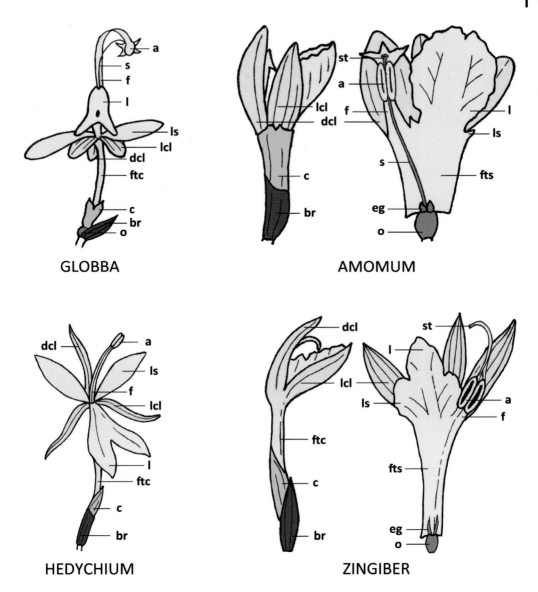

Fig. 4.9 | Diagrammatic flower structure of *Globba, Amomum, Hedychium* and *Zingiber*. Dark green—bracteole (br); light green—calyx (c); red — epigynous glands (eg), ovary (o), style (s), stigma (st); yellow—anther (a), filament (f), staminodial inner part of floral tube (fts), labellum (l), lateral staminodes (ls); orange—outer part of floral tube formed by corolla (ftc), dorsal corolla lobe (dcl), lateral corolla lobe (lcl).

The single functional ginger stamen is composed of a filament and anther. The filament may be so short as to be almost absent, as in some *Zingiber* species or just a few millimetres long but, in *Hedychium*, it may be several centimetres long. In *Globba* and *Gagnepainia* the filament is strongly arched. The anther is composed of

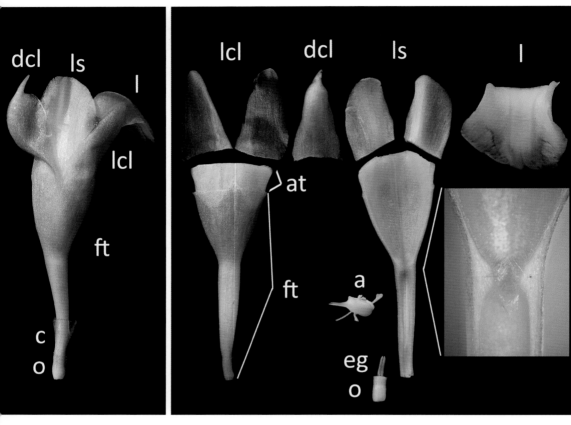

Fig.4.10 *Curcuma* flower from side (left) and dissected (right): a—anther, at— androecial /staminodial tube, c—calyx, dcl—dorsal corolla lobe, eg—epigynous glands, ft—floral tube, l—labellum, lcl—lateral corolla lobes, ls—lateral staminodes, o—ovary.

two parallel pollen sacs or thecae which open towards the inside of the flower, and a highly expanded sterile tissue called the connective which is negligible in many other monocots. In some genera, the connective is prolonged beyond the pollen sacs to produce a structure at the apex of the anther known as the anther crest which may be small and simple (*Curcuma*), wrapped around the stigma to form a horn-like structure (*Zingiber*) or elaborate with lobes and horns (*Amomum* and *Elettariopsis*) or even collar-like and strongly reflexed (*Monolophus*). In *Globba* the structures formed on the sides of the anther thecae are known as lateral appendages, while those formed at the base of the anther thecae e.g. in *Curcuma* and *Roscoea* are called anther spurs. In most genera, the anther is basifixed but, in *Cautleya* and *Curcuma*, the anther is dorsifixed and versatile. The shape of the anther, the presence and shape of the anther crest, spurs and lateral appendages are considered good characters for distinguishing a number of genera, such as *Globba*, *Amomum* and *Curcuma*.

Fig. 4.11 Anthers in Alpinioideae (upper row from left): *Alpinia calcicola*, *Etlingera* sp., *Amomum rubidum*, *Siliquamomum alcicorne*, *Geostachys* aff. *annamensis*. Anthers in Globbeae and Zingibereae (lower row from left): *Globba expansa*, *Monolophus tamdaoensis*, *Curcuma flammea*, *Hedychium* aff. *forrestii*, *Zingiber* sp.

The style is long, thin and thread-like. It runs up the floral tube to the anther where it is held between the two anther thecae and ends in the stigma. This character is found in all Zingiberaceae and Costaceae but in no other plant families. The stigma in some species (mostly in Alpinioideae) moves during the day in order to prevent self-pollination, a phenomenon called flexistyly. The stigma opening is called the ostiole and is almost always ciliate.

The epigynous glands, also known as epigynous nectaries or stylodial glands, produce nectar to attract the pollinators and are found inside the floral tube at the top of the ovary. There are usually two symmetrical glands which can be short or long, sharp or blunt at the apex but, in some species, the two glands merge into one large gland or split into many hair-like glands. Their colour varies from cream, ochreous, and yellowish to yellowish-green. Epigynous glands are present in most ginger genera but are reduced for example in *Newmania* and *Curcuma* subg. *Hitcheniopsis*.

The ovary of gingers is always inferior. Its shape varies from globular to cylindrical and its surface may be smooth or ridged, hairy or glabrous. It may be unilocular with parietal placentation as in *Globba* but, in most genera, it is trilocular with axile placentation. The septation may not always be complete in the upper part of the ovary and, in such cases, this region appears to be unilocular and the placentation more or less free-central (basal). This is found in some species of *Boesenbergia*, *Curcuma*, *Kaempferia* and *Monolophus*.

FRUITS & SEEDS

The fruit is often termed a capsule but this is an oversimplification. There are capsules in the family which may be thin-walled or fleshy, dehiscing by valves or just tearing irregularly. Some species in the Alpinioideae (e.g. *Amomum*, *Etlingera*, *Hornstedtia*), however, produce indehiscent fruits which cannot be called capsules. Following the most recent classification of fruit types, those indehiscent fruits derived from ovaries with septa should be called hesperidia.

The seeds are round, ovoid or narrowly ovoid, sometimes angled. The colour ranges from green, light brown to dark brown, red or dark maroon to almost black. They may be glabrous and shiny, striate or of matt appearance, or shortly hairy. All ginger seeds are arillate. The aril, which is a fleshy appendage positioned at the base of the seed, is often white or light yellow but sometimes bright red (e.g. *Hedychium*), very small (e.g. *Cautleya gracilis*) or well-developed. A well-developed aril may be laciniate, free to the base or only partly, or fully enclose the seed. In some species (e.g. *Alpinia*, *Etlingera*) the aril has a pleasant sweet or sour taste.

Fig. 4.12 Examples of fruits (from left): *Globba* capsule dehiscing by valves; *Gagnepainia* capsule irregularly dehiscing from base; *Siliquamomum* capsule regularly dehiscing by three valves, *Amomum* indehiscent hesperidium.

How to collect gingers

Gingers are a taxonomically challenging group, partly because their delicate floral parts make very poor herbarium specimens. This makes them extremely difficult to identify from dried herbarium material, unless a great deal of care has been invested in its preparation.

To collect a good specimen requires knowledge of the family in order to preserve certain characters important for identification, as well as diligence in preparing good notes with detailed descriptions of characters which will be lost or invisible on the dried specimen.

Many gingers are large plants and it is tempting to collect younger, smaller individuals. This can be misleading, however, and should be avoided. If the leafy shoot is too large to be reasonably folded on a herbarium sheet, then it will have to be mounted over a number of sheets. The base of the pseudostem (including some roots), the middle part of the leafy shoot with well-preserved ligules and the tip of the leafy shoot should be collected. Each of these parts must be clearly labelled in the field or it may be extremely difficult to match the correct parts, and a mixed collection may result. Characters of the leafy shoot which should be noted are its height, how many leaves it has and whether the leaves are distributed evenly along the entire pseudostem, or unevenly, restricted to the upper portion of the pseudostem.

A complete inflorescence attached to the plant should be collected, so that it can clearly be seen whether it arises from the top of the leafy shoot or from the rhizome. Very thick

Fig. 5.1 | Bracts and flowers of *Zingiber nudicarpum* ready to be preserved in 70% ethanol or FAA.

Fig. 5.2 | Bulky inflorescences and infructescences should be sliced in half before drying.

inflorescences or infructescences can be carefully sliced in half. Excess water and mucilage, often found in *Curcuma* and *Zingiber*, can be gently squeezed out and dried with newspapers or paper towels before the specimen is pressed.

As it is extremely hard to preserve dried flowers and even the best-prepared specimens lose their three-dimensional structure, the best practice is always to preserve some flowering and fruiting material in liquid. In the field, alcohol (ethanol) diluted with clean water to 70% is most often used. Later, these collections can be transferred into one of a number of liquid preserving media such as Kew mixture, Copenhagen mixture or FAA. An entire inflorescence, including several single flowers

Fig. 5.3 Taking notes, tagging plants and documenting collections with photographs are best done directly in the field as ginger flowers wilt quickly.

with their subtending bracts and bracteoles, should be preserved. A longitudinal half or quarter of large inflorescences or infructescences may be preserved, or at least several bracts with complete cincinni. All bottles should be clearly labelled with the collection number inside the bottle, using thick archive paper and a dark pencil.

In the current age of digital cameras, it is easier than ever to document plants in the field, at a very low cost. Detailed photographic documentation of gingers should include photographs of the habitat, habit, the base of the plant including its rhizome, root tubers and internal colour, which is particularly important in *Curcuma*, *Kaempferia* and *Zingiber*. Photographs of the leaves should include shots of both

2 cm

0.5 cm

Fig. 5.4 | A photo-document of *Distichochlamys rubrostriata* showing front and side views of the flower, a dissection of the flower, close-up details of the anther from all sides, and epigynous glands.

sides, ligules (preferably from various parts of the leafy shoot as their shape and size depend on their position on the leafy shoot in certain species), pulvinus if present, petioles, base and apex of the leaf. The origin of the inflorescence and its peduncle should be clearly recorded. The flowers should be photographed from the front and side. A flower dissection on a neutral background (black synthetic velvet usually being the best option) is time-consuming but offers invaluable information about the floral structures and their dimensions and is becoming a standard part of a ginger description, particularly of a new taxon.

Once pressed, herbarium specimens can be dried in the field or preserved in liquid, packed in several layers of thick polyethylene bags, and processed a few weeks later. Each method has its advantages and disadvantages.

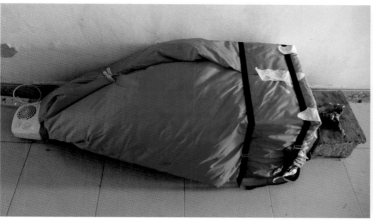

Fig. 5.5 A field dryer, made of a herbarium press, a heater fan and a large plastic bag can dry most specimens in 24—36 hours.

The 'wet method' or 'Schweinfurth method', which preserves specimens in a liquid such as diluted alcohol or formaldehyde, is sometimes the only option in very remote areas, where there is no electricity, or the construction of a field drier is not practical. It also saves time in the field. The main disadvantage of this method is that the specimens lose all their colour and often turn dark. Furthermore, DNA cannot be taken from them. A large supply of preserving liquid is needed and the bundles of preserved specimens become rather heavy.

Drying specimens in the field is laborious but often results in better specimens, particularly when electricity is easily available. An effective drier can easily be made by using a small heater fan (such as an ordinary hairdryer), large, thick polyethylene or waterproof textile bag and the usual press ends, cardboard and newspaper.

The importance of collecting duplicates of each collection cannot be overstated. Duplicate collections can be distributed to a number of herbaria which, in turn, greatly increases the chances of the specimens being seen and identified. They also confer a degree of insurance; if a specimen at one herbarium should be damaged, there are duplicates preserved elsewhere.

With the advancement of molecular methods, the collection of DNA samples has become a routine part of botanical collecting. Specimens processed by wet methods are unsuitable for DNA study and, even in dried specimens, the DNA is often degraded, depending on the temperature and speed of the drying process. Finely shredded leaf samples placed in clearly labelled teabags and dried quickly in plentiful silica gel in an airtight container are the best way to collect DNA samples in the field. When picking a leaf, avoid collecting the youngest or oldest leaves. The second or third youngest leaves are often the best as they are usually still pest free, yet the frantic enzymatic activity connected with rapid growth of the youngest leaves, which sometimes inhibits DNA extraction, has already ceased.

Fig. 5.6 A tired but happy expedition team with its catch of the day, *Curcuma flammea*, a recently described species from the Vang Vieng limestone, Laos.

Reproductive biology

Plants are often capable of two types of reproduction, vegetative and sexual, which differ greatly in their effect on the evolution of species. Vegetative reproduction is essentially maintenance of a fixed genetic type with very little possibility of variation upon which natural selection may act. On the other hand, sexual reproduction, involving pollination and seed dispersal, mixes genes, producing variation which may lead to continued existence or to extinction of a genetic type. Much remains to be learned about the reproductive biology of Zingiberaceae, particularly in Cambodia, Laos and Vietnam. This kind of work can really only be done in the field so it is better done by researchers who live near the places where natural populations occur.

SEXUAL REPRODUCTION

All Zingiberaceae have complex, zygomorphic flowers which last less than a single day or, at most, two to three days. This suggests a close relationship between each plant species and one or a few species of pollinator. So far five flower types have been described in gingers but more may yet be recognised.

Tubular flowers are characterised by a long, narrow floral tube without spreading corolla lobes or labellum. Examples of tubular flowers can be seen in some *Renealmia* species in South America, which are hummingbird-pollinated, and in *Rhynchanthus, Etlingera* and *Hornstedtia* in Asia, which are also bird pollinated.

Exposed flowers are open and have the limb of the labellum spreading horizontally.

Fig. 6.1 | Tubular flower type, *Hornstedtia incana.*

Fig. 6.2 | Exposed flower type, *Alpinia aquatica* (left) and *Alpinia galanga* (right).

Fig. 6.3 | Gullet flower type, *Curcuma codonantha* (left) and *Amomum xanthophlebium* (right).

Flowers of this type may be seen, for example, in some *Alpinia* species, and in *Renealmia* in South America. They are bee-pollinated.

In **gullet flowers**, the floral parts form a broad chamber, as seen for example in *Alpinia zerumbet* and its relatives, some *Amomum* species, *Camptandra*, *Cautleya*, *Curcuma* and *Roscoea* which are thought to be bee-pollinated.

The **elongate flower** type is close to the exposed type. The main difference is that the anther and the entrance to the floral tube are far apart, e.g. *Globba*, *Hedychium*. These flowers may be pollinated by bees or lepidopterans (moths and butterflies).

Fig. 6.4 Elongate flower type, *Hedychium roxburghii* (left), *Globba saltatoria* (right).

Fig. 6.5 | Planar flower type, *Kaempferia pulchra* (left), and *Haplochorema* sp. (right).

Planar flowers have a flat face as seen for example in *Kaempferia*. These flowers are believed to be pollinated by lepidopterans (moths and butterflies).

Pollination by hummingbirds has been well-documented in tropical America. There are no hummingbirds in Asia but sunbirds and spiderhunters are known to feed on

Fig. 6.6 | Purple-throated Carib hummingbird pollinating a flower of *Heliconia caribea* (left), little spiderhunter pollinating *Etlingera elatior* (right).

REPRODUCTIVE BIOLOGY

Fig. 6.7 Hovering crimson sunbird pollinating *Thalia dealbata,* an introduced ornamental plant in Singapore.

nectar and effect pollination of various *Etlingera* and *Hornstedtia* species, which have long, tubular flowers that are relatively tough and resistant to damage caused by a bird's beak.

Two genera in Cambodia, Laos and Vietnam, *Cautleya* and *Curcuma*, and two more further afield, *Camptandra* and *Roscoea*, have truly versatile anthers with basal spurs approximately at right angles to the thecae and lying across the entry to the floral tube. When a flower visitor pushes its head into the flower, the anther works like a hinge, turning and depositing pollen on the back of the visitor. This is known as the *Salvia*-mechanism, after the genus in which it was first observed. It has been observed that bees are the pollinators of at least some of the species in these genera.

REPRODUCTIVE BIOLOGY

Fig. 6.8 Examples of bee pollination in flowers without versatile anthers; *Zingiber nudicarpum* in Laos (left) and *Alpinia aquatica* in Singapore (right).

Bees have also been seen to pollinate some *Alpinia*, *Amomum*, *Globba* and *Zingiber* which do not have versatile anthers. Small butterflies are also seen visiting *Globba* flowers occasionally though it is not known whether they can pollinate them.

The flowers of *Hedychium* are often scented and flower at night. The floral tube is long so the pollinator must have a long tongue. It is thought that the pollinators will be moths and butterflies. The same may be true of the night-flowering *Kaempferia* species, such as *K. fallax*. Beyond Cambodia, Laos and Vietnam, there are species of *Alpinia*, *Curcuma* and *Leptosolena* which flower at night. These species usually have a long floral tube and white or yellow flowers. Some are sweetly scented while others have a strong, musty smell.

There are almost no published records of seed dispersal in Zingiberaceae though it seems almost certain that dispersal is carried out by animals, rather than inanimate agents, such as wind or water. The strongest verifiable evidence comes from camera-traps set in a number of sites in Singapore. These show that the seeds of three species of *Hornstedtia* are dispersed by rodents and squirrels, and by macaques which open the fruits to eat the seeds.

Fig. 6.9 | Elongate flower type, *Hedychium longicornutum* visited by a butterfly.

A curious method of dispersal has been observed in Africa by D. J. Harris. Here, a species of *Aframomum* flowers in muddy soil near water. The fruits form in the soil which bakes hard in the sun during the dry season. At the next rainy season, the mud is softened in the rising waters, and fish come to eat the fruits.

Further discussion of dispersal is based on the characters of the fruits and what is known of the preferences of dispersing agents. The fruits of *Hedychium*, for example, open when they are ripe to reveal a bright orange inner fruit wall and a mass of seeds covered in a bright red aril. It is known that birds find these colours attractive. Similarly, the inner fruit wall of *Zingiber* is bright red, the seeds are shiny black and the aril, which only partially covers the seeds, is white. These fruits generally occur near ground level and may be eaten by rodents and other small mammals.

Fig. 6.10 Ripe fruits of *Zingiber* aff. *teres* (left) and *Hedychium erythrostemon* (right).

Fig. 6.11 Ripe fruits of *Hornstedtia sanhan*. The seeds are embedded in a fragrant and sour-sweet tasting aril.

The aril of ginger seeds is rich in nutrients, often strongly scented and sweet or sour tasting so even indehiscent fruits, such as those of *Amomum* may be chewed open by small mammals in search of food. In Sulawesi, some species of *Etlingera* produce large heads of tough fruits which are said to be eaten by the anoa, an endemic mammal related to cattle. In Cambodia, Laos and Vietnam, wild boar may be attracted by the fruits of gingers.

There is evidence from the Neotropics that ants disperse arillate seeds of the related plant family Marantaceae. Ants have also been seen to drag away the seeds of some species of *Curcuma* and *Globba* in Asia.

VEGETATIVE REPRODUCTION

All gingers have a rhizome which allows the plant to persist. In many species, the rhizome branches frequently, producing either a clump of many pseudostems or a spreading colony. Typical clump-forming species in Cambodia, Laos and Vietnam are *Alpinia galanga* and *Hedychium* spp. while the spreading form is shown by *Amomum uliginosum* and *Etlingera megalocheilos*. Many species of *Curcuma* have much-branched and sometimes also running rhizomes, which easily break off and give rise to new plants well away from the mother plant.

Bulbils are small shoots which become detached easily from the mother plant and begin to grow if they fall on suitable ground. They are most often seen in certain species of *Globba* such as *G. marantina* and *G. schomburgkii*. Some species of *Alpinia* also produce a kind of bulbil which looks like a small plant growing out of an old inflorescence.

A third type of vegetative reproduction is shown by a few species of *Zingiber* and *Newmania*, which have long, arching leafy shoots. These may bend down to touch the ground where they take root and begin to grow.

Fig. 6.12 | *Globba schomburgkii* with bulbils (left); *Zingiber singapurense* (right) with a young plantlet at the apex of the leafy shoot.

Fig. 6.13 Gregariously fruiting *Zingiber teres* can be seen in early December in Tam Đào National Park, Vietnam.

Ecology

Most gingers grow in the shade of taller plants, mainly under trees in forest. Very few can tolerate full sun. Rather little is known of the ecology of individual species of gingers but it is possible to discern groups of species which are each associated with a different habitat type.

LOWLAND EVERGREEN FOREST

This type of forest is found at altitudes from sea level to about 1000 m. The rainy season is very wet and the humidity high throughout the year. Usually, the soil is rich and, for this reason, most of this forest type has been replaced by agriculture. The majority of the woody species growing here are evergreen and may reach 30–35 m tall. Some grow on the banks of streams, where they may be flooded. This habitat type can be seen, for example, at Mount Hòn Bà, Núi Chúa National Park and Kon Ka Kinh National Park, Vietnam; Champasak Province, Laos and Posat Province, Cambodia.

Many species of gingers are found in this habitat; they belong to the following genera: *Alpinia*, *Amomum*, *Distichochlamys*, *Elettariopsis*, *Etlingera*, *Gagnepainia*, *Geostachys*, *Globba*, *Hornstedtia* and *Zingiber*.

Fig. 7.1 Lowland evergreen forest at about 800 m on Mount Hòn Bà, southern Vietnam.

Fig. 7.2 | Montane forest in Hòn Bà Nature Reserve, southern Vietnam.

EVERGREEN MONTANE FOREST

At more than 1000 m above sea level, the forest is usually evergreen and lacks the tropical elements of the lowlands, such as Dipterocarpaceae, Euphorbiaceae and Meliaceae. In places it is composed of broadleaved species alone, while elsewhere, there may be a significant proportion of conifers. Species in the broadleaved families Lauraceae and Fagaceae are particularly abundant.

The following genera of gingers commonly occur in this forest: *Cautleya*, *Elettariopsis*, *Geostachys*, *Hedychium*, *Siliquamomum* and *Zingiber*.

On ridges and towards the summits of mountains from 600–1900 m above sea level, where the temperature is cool, 10–15° C in winter, the dominant trees are pines and other conifers. In Cambodia, this forest type can be found in Kirirom National Park at 600–700 m altitude, with *Curcuma sparganifolia* and *Curcuma singularis* growing in *Vietnamosasa* grassland under pines. At higher elevation, 1500–1900 m, it can be

Fig. 7.3 | Evergreen montane forest in Tam Đảo National Park, northern Vietnam.

ECOLOGY

Fig. 7.4 Pine forest with *Vietnamosasa* grassland in Kirirom National Park, Cambodia (above); pine forest on Mount Lang Bian with *Hedychium* and *Zingiber* species in the undergrowth (below).

ECOLOGY

Fig. 7.5 | Limestone at Vang Vieng, Laos.

found on Mount Lang Bian in Vietnam, where species of *Zingiber* and *Hedychium*, which prefer moisture and cool temperatures, occur. The soil here is rich and sandy.

In evergreen forest at all altitudes, there are some *Hedychium* species which grow as epiphytes. They have been found at Khelee Vongkhot, Champasak Province, Laos and in Đà Lạt, Lâm Đồng Province, Vietnam, growing on trees in forests with high humidity and cool temperatures.

FOREST ON LIMESTONE

Rocky outcrops can be found in grassland and dry forest from the lowlands to the high mountains (c. 1600 m above sea level). These include the famous karst landscapes of SE Asia. Various forest types occur, depending on local conditions. The forest may be evergreen or semi-deciduous, consisting of broadleaved trees or a mixture of broadleaved trees and conifers.

Certain genera of gingers are more common on limestone. *Boesenbergia* spp., *Kaempferia* spp. and *Hedychium* spp., for example, grow on large rocks near water in deep shade or with moss in shallow pockets of soil among rocks in full sun.

Fig. 7.6 | Limestone at Vang Vieng, Laos (left) and Xuân Sơn National Park, Vietnam (right).

SEMI-DECIDUOUS & DECIDUOUS DRY LOWLAND FOREST

This habitat usually occurs under scattered deciduous trees in the Dipterocarpaceae at 0–500 (700) m above sea level. In Africa and the Neotropics, it would be called savanna. The rainy season lasts four to five months from the end of May to September and the annual rainfall is less than 2000 mm. The soil is generally sandy, free-draining and poor. There is a ground layer of herbs, mainly grasses. Dry dipterocarp forest can be found, for example, in Lò Gò-Xa Mát National Park, Tây Ninh Province, Vietnam; in Khong district, Champasak Province, Laos and in Veal Veng district, Posat Province, Cambodia.

The species which occur in this habitat are almost all deciduous, meaning that they completely die back to the underground rhizome during the dry season. Species preferring this habitat are *Curcuma alismatifolia, C. gracillima, C. petiolata, C. pierreana, C. thorelii, Globba adhaerens, Kaempferia champasakensis, K. galanga,*

Fig. 7.7 | Semi-deciduous dry forest in Lò Gò-Xa Mát National Park, southern Vietnam.

K. fallax, *Zingiber pellitum* and *Z. junceum*. Each species has its own tolerance to sunlight, *Globba adhaerens* grows in shade, while *Kaempferia fallax* and *Curcuma thorelii* are found in full sun in very short grass. The remaining species have neutral tolerance to the light; they either grow in the forest margin, or in long grass.

Gallery forest is an evergreen forest type found along watercourses which run through dry forests. Some *Alpinia* species grow on stream banks and in flooded areas in gallery forest.

COASTAL VEGETATION & LOWLAND WETLANDS

Very few ginger species are found in these habitat types. *Alpinia conchigera* is sometimes found in wetlands, and *Curcuma arida* grows in Núi Chúa National Park, Ninh Thuận, Vietnam.

Fig. 7.8 The view from the 1450 m peak of Bạch Mã National Park, central Vietnam (above); coastal vegetation in Núi Chúa National Park, southern Vietnam (below).

ECOLOGY

Conservation

Cambodia, Laos and Vietnam are changing fast. The human population is growing rapidly in number and incomes are also growing, resulting in considerable pressure on the environment. During such a phase of development, policy decisions will be taken which will result in some destruction of the environment in return for immediate benefits to the population. The value of these short-term benefits must be weighed against the long-term health of the ecosystem because we are all part of the world's ecosystem and our long-term survival depends upon it. Information is needed in order to make these decisions but, in Cambodia, Laos and Vietnam, this information on natural systems is often incomplete or lacking.

Some of the information needed to make wise decisions is relatively easy to come by. It is a matter of measuring and observing natural phenomena such as the names, distributions and ecology of species or their market value. This can only be done if there are enough trained scientists to carry out the work which is not the case in Cambodia, Laos and Vietnam.

Fig. 8.1 | Quarrying of limestone causes serious and irreversible damage to the ecosystem.

Fig. 8.2 Limestone karsts, such as these in Kien Giang province in southern Vietnam, are very rich in biodiversity.

Fig. 8.3 Floral arrangements and whole plants of *Curcuma sparganiifolia* dug out with rhizomes can be seen on sale in Kirirom National Park in Cambodia. The local people do not realise that repeated harvesting of rhizomes will eventually deplete the entire population and that ex-situ propagation of ornamental species would provide them with a more sustainable livelihood.

In other ways, though, it is much more difficult to quantify the value of nature. The forest and its animals play a very strong role in the cultures of Cambodia, Laos and Vietnam but it is difficult to quantify this effect. What would it be like to live in a world with a much reduced number of species, where the call of the hornbill or the gibbon was no longer heard and the colour and fragrance of many flower species could no longer be appreciated? We should certainly be impoverished to a degree, though we might survive at a material level.

The area of natural vegetation in Cambodia, Laos and Vietnam is declining rapidly. This is a worldwide phenomenon and, indeed, we are living through a period of extinction greater than any known before. According to a report called Plants under Pressure written at the Royal Botanic Gardens, Kew and first published in 2010, more than 20% of plants are threatened with extinction. This measure does not take into account species which have not yet been described. At a conservative estimate, there are more species still to be described than those we know already, most of them in groups such as arthropods and protozoa but also plenty of vascular plants in tropical countries.

CONSERVATION

Fig. 8.4 | Slash-and-burn agriculture which rapidly clears large portions of primary forests, is common in all three countries.

In an effort to protect species, the Parties to the Convention on Biological Diversity committed themselves, in April 2002, to achieving by 2010 a significant reduction of the current rate of biodiversity loss at the global, regional and national level as a contribution to poverty alleviation and to the benefit of all life on Earth. All 190 signatories to this agreement missed the target.

CONSERVATION

Fig. 8.5 Capacity training in the region is one way to increase awareness of biodiversity, and to give local botanists the skills needed to conserve it.

On a more positive note, each government has created a system of forest reserves where plants and animals receive a degree of protection. There are about 50 national parks in Cambodia, Laos and Vietnam, 7 in Cambodia, 23 in Laos and 30 in Vietnam. Aiichi Biodiversity Target 11 calls for protected areas to encompass 17% of terrestrial ecosystems in each country. Cambodia and Laos have surpassed this target but Vietnam is only about halfway there, according to the Asia Protected Planet Report published in 2014. Of course, the degree of protection afforded to plants and animals in these parks is not always very high.

One factor in the discussion of biodiversity loss is the taxonomic impediment, namely the lack of trained taxonomists working to document the world's species. The Global Taxonomic Initiative aims to remove the taxonomic impediment by training more taxonomists and by making information available through the internet. This book addresses the same problem by encouraging people in Cambodia, Laos and Vietnam to look more closely at the plants which grow around them and to conserve them for the future.

A category of threat can be assigned to a species according to the system devised and run by the International Union for the Conservation of Nature (IUCN). Quite a lot of detailed information is required to make a full assessment of the threat to a species, most of it not yet known for the species of Zingiberaceae in Cambodia, Laos and Vietnam. IUCN has published assessments of 35 species of *Amomum* and of one or two recently published species but the majority of species cannot yet be assessed. These species are treated as data deficient at the moment.

Of the species which have been assessed, many are threatened to some degree. The threat can come from reduction in the area of occupation of the species, or disturbance of the areas where it grows. Some species, like the newly described *Curcuma vitellina*, are only known from one or two sites in Vietnam so any disturbance to these sites can be very damaging. The preliminary assessment of *C. vitellina* indicates that it has a small area of occupancy, being found at only two sites in Lâm Đồng Province where erosion and development for tourism are reducing the quality of the habitat. It has been assessed as Critically Endangered C2a(i). Another example is *Amomum petaloideum*, a species originally described from Mengla County, Yunnan Province, China. This species was first discovered in Laos in 2008 but, by 2009, the area where it was found had been cleared and planted with rubber. *Amomum petaloideum* is globally assessed as Vulnerable A2ac but no new populations have been located in the area of Laos in which it was found in 2008, and it may be nationally extinct.

One of the threats to plants is an inadequate legal framework which doesn't regulate the collection of plants in national parks in a way that ensures that species are not overcollected or put in danger of extinction. Another threat arises from widespread ignorance or deliberate breaking of existing laws. This latter threat can only be countered by increased efforts to teach the general public the meaning of the law, and the value of conserving plants for the future.

It has to be admitted that, at the moment, the future for many plant species is uncertain. Efforts are under way to conserve them but they may come too late. It is greatly to be hoped that the people of Cambodia, Laos and Vietnam will find ways to ensure their economic development without losing too much of their biodiversity.

CONSERVATION

Fig. 8.6 | *Curcuma vitellina* is a critically endangered species recently described from southern Vietnam.

Ethnobotany

Many ginger species are used in the daily lives of people in Cambodia, Laos and Vietnam. They are an important source of food, food colourings, herbs and spices, flavouring agents, medicines and ornamentals, both for home use and for trade, giving them a significant economic value. In addition, certain species of *Alpinia, Amomum, Curcuma, Etlingera, Globba, Kaempferia* and *Zingiber* are used in religious ceremonies and for other cultural purposes.

SPICES & CONDIMENTS

Ginger (*Zingiber officinale*), turmeric (*Curcuma longa*) and cardamom (*Elettaria cardamomum*) are not only the best known members of the ginger family, but also economically the most important ones. Together with greater galangal (*Alpinia galanga*) and fingerroot (*Boesenbergia rotunda*), these spices are highly valued and used in numerous food preparations to add flavour and to balance the meal. Like many east Asian peoples, the Vietnamese follow a concept originating from traditional Chinese medicine, which recognises the need for balance between ying and yang in order to maintain good health. According to this concept, foods are classified into heating (yang, inducing hot energy in the body), cooling (ying, inducing cold energy) and neutral. *Ginger* is "heating" so it is used to cook with chicken, a "cooling" meat. *Alpinia galanga* is almost always cooked with dog meat. Other uses of Zingiberaceae in Vietnamese cuisine are in *phở*, a nourishing beef noodle dish which is spiced with ginger and at times also with some *Amomum* species. Vietnamese people also frequently eat ginger in hot and cold desserts, and preserve it as candied ginger called *mứt*.

In Cambodia, turmeric and ginger, fresh or as a dried powder, are often added to curries, soups and stir-fried dishes. The rhizomes of *Boesenbergia rotunda* are indispensable in curry pastes, particularly the famous fish amok, but they are also used in stir-frying. *Alpinia galanga*, greater galangal, is extensively used in Khmer cuisine. When the rhizome is young, it is best used in soups, while more pungent, mature rhizomes are used in curries and stir-fried dishes.

Fig. 9.1 Fish amok (left), a typical Cambodian dish, uses turmeric while stir-fried beef with red tree ants is spiced with greater galangal.

Although the true cardamom (*Elettaria cardamomum*) does not occur in Cambodia, Laos and Vietnam, the dried fruit and seeds of various species of *Amomum,* often called wild cardamom, are of great economic value in these countries. Wild cardamom is among the most valuable of all Lao export products, representing 60-70% of the total export value of non-timber forest products and is collected almost exclusively for export to China, Korea and Thailand, sometimes via traders in Vietnam.

Fig. 9.2 Dried fruits of *Amomum verum* are easily available in markets in Phnom Penh.

FRUIT, VEGETABLES & STARCH

Fresh ripe fruits of *Amomum dealbatum* have a sweet taste and can be found at local markets in northern Laos or at the central market of Louangprabang, when in season.

In Laos, *Alpinia galanga*, is very popular not only as a flavouring, but also as a vegetable and can be bought in any market. Rhizomes, young shoots and inflorescences are all eaten. Young inflorescences of certain *Zingiber* species are stir-fried and eaten as vegetables. Lao and Vietnamese people enjoy eating fresh salad leaves, among them the leaves of *Kaempferia* species which are rolled up and dipped in sauces.

In Vietnam young inflorescences and leafy shoots of some *Curcuma* species are added to soups, and young leaves of some other gingers, such as *Kaempferia*, are eaten raw as an accompaniment to noodle dishes. The rhizomes of *Curcuma* species are very rich in starch which may be extracted and consumed with sugar or honey in the form of a thick, warm drink, or the whole fresh rhizomes may be pounded and boiled into a starchy porridge.

Fig. 9.3 Salads made of fresh leaves, some of them gingers, are often served in Laos and Vietnam

Fig. 9.4 Inflorescences of *Curcuma pambrosima,* native to Central Vietnam, are sold at markets and used in the preparation of soups.

MEDICINAL USES

Throughout Cambodia, Laos and Vietnam, the rhizomes of numerous species of *Alpinia*, *Curcuma*, *Kaempferia* and *Zingiber* as well as fruits and seeds of *Amomum* species are sold in traditional medicine shops and markets.

In Cambodia, the rhizome of *Alpinia* is used as a stimulant, antitussive, diaphoretic, and a moderator of uterine haemorrhage. It may be used internally, against liver disease, and for curing chronic bronchitis, or externally against liver disease, neuralgia and rheumatism.

In Laos, the young rhizomes of *Alpinia galanga* are used for curing rashes and skin disease. The rhizomes are cut into slices, salted, lightly toasted and then applied to the affected skin. Lao people also make tinctures of wild cardamom fruits and seeds (various species of *Amomum*) which they drink to treat stomach ache or use in other traditional cures. The spicy seeds of *A. sericeum* and *A. villosum* are used for reducing the pain of toothache. *Amomum villosum* is also used in Laos and Vietnam to treat stomach problems, constipation, dysentery, and other digestive problems.

In Vietnam, the common ginger, *Zingiber officinale*, is used in many ways to relieve various illnesses and discomforts. Rice porridge with ginger is a typical food served to ill people. Ginger is also brewed with tea or just with honey and lemon, to treat coughs and to warm the body in cold weather. Crushed ginger is also used to massage

Fig. 9.5 Baskets overflowing with a variety of ginger rhizomes are a common sight in Cambodia (above) and Vietnam (below).

ETHNOBOTANY

Fig. 9.6 Fruits of unidentified *Amomum,* locally called *sa nhân,* are sold by Raglai people in southern Vietnam. They are pickled in alcohol and used to relieve backache.

bruises and swellings to make them heal faster. Ginger medicated oil can be purchased for relieving vomiting, diarrhoea, rheumatism, or preventing cold.

Turmeric, *Curcuma longa,* is mixed with honey, and both turmeric and ginger are used to treat stomach ailments. Likewise, in An Giang province, some species of *Curcuma* are cultivated for treating stomach ache. The dried rhizomes of about 5–8 species of *Curcuma* are powdered and drunk with fresh water or mixed with honey. Turmeric and other *Curcuma* species with deep orange rhizomes are also popular ingredients in soaps, creams and facial scrubs produced by local companies. Vietnamese people also pickle rhizomes and fruits of various species (e.g. *Kaempferia, Amomum*) in alcohol for extended periods and the resulting tincture is used in massage to cure backaches. Tincture of *Kaempferia rotunda* is also used to treat snake bites.

CHILDBIRTH & POSTPARTUM
Many ethnic groups in Laos practise confinement of mothers after childbirth in a "hot bed", that's to say a closed room with a fire which is kept very warm for the post-partum period. During this time of 10–15 days, the only food that the mother may eat, along with plain sticky rice, is the young rhizome of *Alpinia galanga,* washed, sliced into thin pieces, salted and then fried or toasted. Also during this hot confinement, leaves and leaf sheaths of *Alpinia galanga* are boiled with other aromatic plants

Fig. 9.7 | A mixture of herbs, topped with dried slices of *Curcuma zanthorrhiza,* used in a medicinal steam-bath (Cambodia).

to make a steam-bath or a sauna. This type of steam-bath is also used by people generally to cure headaches and fevers. *Amomum microcarpum*, *A. uliginosum* and *A. villosum* are also used in a herbal mixture for medicinal saunas or steam-baths, in the same way as *Alpinia galanga*, during confinement after childbirth, and generally for curing headaches and fevers. The whole plant is cleaned, and boiled to make scented, medicinal steam.

In Cambodia, the seeds of *Amomum verum* are also used medicinally by mothers after childbirth. The seeds are boiled, and the decoction drunk as a tonic, to eliminate internal poisons or to treat haemorrhages.

DYES
Food may be coloured and flavoured using the rhizome of turmeric (*Curcuma longa*). Holy water is made from the sliced rhizomes of turmeric and is used in local culture and religion. Traditionally, Buddhist monks used turmeric to dye their orange robes but, nowadays, artificial dyes, which are more stable and long-lasting, have replaced this custom. Sometimes other *Curcuma* species with bright orange rhizomes, such as *C. zanthorrhiza*, may be used instead.

ETHNOBOTANY

Fig. 9.8 | A plantation of *Alpinia galanga* in northern Laos.

Genera to be expected

The genera which are known to occur in Cambodia, Laos and Vietnam have been presented in some detail but there are still a few genera which seem likely to occur in the area although they have not yet been found. Three such genera, *Cornukaempferia*, *Pommereschea* and *Rhynchanthus*, are found in neighbouring countries, China and Thailand, in forest types which also occur in Cambodia, Laos and Vietnam, and are therefore briefly described and illustrated here.

CORNUKAEMPFERIA

This genus of three species is endemic to Thailand. *Cornukaempferia larsenii* occurs quite near the Lao-Thai border and may be expected in Laos. *Cornukaempferia* has been reported to grow in mixed deciduous forests or in mature secondary evergreen forest, in humus-rich soils.

Fig. 10.1 | *Cornukaempferia* species have beautiful silver patches on their leaves.

Fig. 10.2 | *Cornukaempferia aurantiflora* (left) and *Cornukaempferia longipetiolata* (right).

Cornukaempferia belongs in the Zingiberoideae tribe Zingibereae and has flowers very like those of *Zingiber* in which the anther crest is long and wrapped round the style like a curved horn. The leaves, however, are much more like those of *Kaempferia*. They are broad, often with patches of silver on top and wine red below; they do not form a pseudostem but rather a loose tuft. The inflorescence is terminal on the tuft.

POMMERESCHEA

This genus, with two known species, is found in northern Burma, northern Thailand and Yunnan so it may yet be found in northern Laos or northern Vietnam. *Pommereschea* has no lateral staminodes so it was classified in the Alpinioideae until molecular phylogenetic evidence revealed a relationship to the genera of the Zingiberoideae. On further investigation, it was found that the plane of distichy of the leaves was parallel to the direction of growth of the rhizome, a character which further supports placing *Pommereschea* in the Zingibereae.

Pommereschea grows in cracks in limestone on high mountains, at around 1000 m altitude. It is a small, deciduous herb, about 30 cm tall with cordate or almost arrow-shaped leaf bases. The inflorescences are terminal on the leafy shoot and the bracts each subtend one flower with a minute bracteole. The labellum is narrow and bifid

Fig. 10.3 | *Pommereschea lackneri* in northern Thailand.

while lateral staminodes are absent. The anther resembles that of *Globba*, being long and arched over the labellum. There is no anther crest and the ovary is trilocular.

RHYNCHANTHUS

This is a genus of 4–5 species found from NE India (Assam) through northern Burma and Thailand to Yunnan. It may be found in northern Laos or northern Vietnam.

These plants are of an extraordinary appearance, resembling *Aeschynanthus* (Gesneriaceae) from a distance, owing to their epiphytic habit, bright red bracts and orange flowers which seem adapted for bird pollination.

Like *Pommereschea*, *Rhynchanthus* has no lateral staminodes, yet it is classified in the Zingibereae because the plane of distichy of the leaves is parallel to the direction of growth of the rhizome. All species grow in cracks in rocks or on trees and have thick rhizomes and roots with which to cling on. The inflorescences are terminal on the leafy shoots and each bright orange to red bract has a single yellow to orange flower. The corolla is long and tubular with short lobes and the labellum is reduced to a small tooth at the base of the long-exserted, concave filament. The anther has no crest and the ovary is trilocular.

Fig. 10.4 | The inflorescence of *Rhynchanthus beesianus* has striking colours which can be seen by birds from far away.

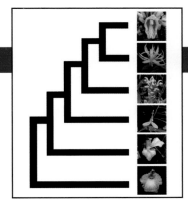

Classification

The genera of gingers have been classified into different groups over the years. The most easily observed characters which have been used to define these groups are the size of the lateral staminodes and the number of locules in the ovary. The first infrafamiliar classification was made by Petersen in the first edition of Engler and Prantl's *Die natürlichen Pflanzenfamilien* of 1889. Petersen recognised three tribes – Globbeae (unilocular ovary), Hedychieae (trilocular ovary and large staminodes) and Zingibereae (trilocular ovary and small staminodes). When Schumann revised all the known species of Zingiberaceae for Engler and Prantl's *Das Pflanzenreich* in 1904, he followed the same classification.

In 1950, Holttum proposed changes to the above system, recognising three tribes named Hedychieae, Alpinieae and Globbeae. He explained that the side-lobes of the labellum in *Zingiber* are, in fact, large lateral staminodes attached to the labellum so he moved *Zingiber* to the Hedychieae and re-named the former tribe Zingibereae Alpinieae. The tribe including the type genus of the family should be called Zingibereae but Holttum hesitated to re-name the well-established Hedychieae after including *Zingiber* in it.

In 1964 Burtt and Smith tentatively suggested that *Zingiber* should be recognised as a separate tribe and further morphological work by Burtt & Olatunji resulted in a division of the family into four tribes, namely Alpinieae, Globbeae, Hedychieae and Zingibereae in 1972. This classification was followed until recently.

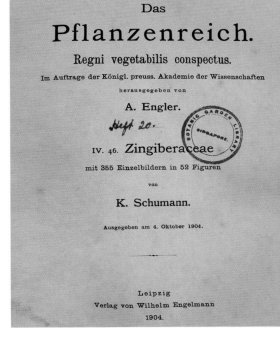

Fig. 11.1 Cover page of Schumann's Zingiberaceae which remains the only comprehensive account of the family.

Fig. 11.2 Brian Lawrence 'Bill' Burtt (left); W. John Kress (right) with a local field guide.

With the arrival of molecular phylogenetic techniques, it became possible to test this classification. Kress and his co-workers, in a paper published in the American Journal of Botany in 2002, carried out a broad study of the genera of gingers, the results of which confirmed many of the groupings established by earlier morphologists. Kress *et al.* did, however, make some adjustments to the ranks of the groups and created a few new ones. This classification, which divides the family into four subfamilies and six tribes, is followed here. The subfamilies and tribes which are found in Cambodia, Laos and Vietnam are indicated with bold font.

Subfamily	Tribe
Siphonochiloideae	Siphonochileae
Tamijioideae	Tamijieae
Alpinioideae	**Alpinieae** Riedelieae
Zingiberoideae	**Zingibereae** **Globbeae**

The following descriptions of subfamilies and tribes, and the characters used in the key to the genera encompass the morphological variation found in Cambodia, Laos and Vietnam only.

Fig. 11.3 Alpinioideae and Globbeae of Cambodia, Laos and Vietnam (from left to right, top to bottom). Alpiniaeae: *Alpinia, Amomum, Elettariopsis, Etlingera, Geostachys, Hornstedtia* and *Siliquamomum*. Globbeae: *Gagnepainia* and *Globba*.

CLASSIFICATION

ALPINIOIDEAE: Alpinieae

The centre of diversity of the Alpinieae is in the evergreen humid tropics, particularly the equatorial zone. Only seven genera are found in Cambodia, Laos and Vietnam. These are medium-sized to large evergreen plants with the plane of distichy of the leafy shoot perpendicular to the fibrous rhizome. The common features of nearly all members of this subfamily are greatly reduced lateral staminodes, which are tooth-like or, less often, heart-shaped or wing-shaped, or completely absent. The ovary is trilocular, developing into an indehiscent fruit (hesperidium) or fleshy dehiscent capsule. Note that the lateral staminodes of *Siliquamomum* are relatively large and, in earlier classifications, this genus was placed in the Zingibereae. Following recent molecular studies *Siliquamomum* is here classified in the Alpinioideae and tentatively placed in the tribe Alpinieae, although morphologically it also has some affinities to the Riedelieae. Its exact position is currently being investigated.

ZINGIBEROIDEAE: Globbeae

Two of the three genera of the Globbeae are represented in Cambodia, Laos and Vietnam. They are small to medium-sized plants rarely exceeding 1 m in height with the plane of distichy of the leafy shoot parallel to the small, fleshy rhizome which often has long root tubers. All species are capable of dormancy though some do not go dormant every year. The lateral staminodes are petaloid and free of the labellum or, sometimes, the lateral staminodes and labellum are adnate to the filament, forming a slender tube. The filament is always longer than the anther and arched. The ovary is unilocular with parietal placentation and turns into a globose, irregularly dehiscent capsule.

ZINGIBEROIDEAE: Zingibereae

The Zingibereae is morphologically the most diverse tribe of the family. The centre of its diversity is in monsoonal Asia with 9 genera represented in Cambodia, Laos and Vietnam. Most members of this tribe are small to medium-sized plants, rarely exceeding 2 m in height, which generally go dormant during the dry period of the year. The plane of distichy of the leafy shoot is parallel to the rhizome, which is fleshy and often well developed with roots often ending in root tubers. The lateral staminodes are petaloid and conspicuous though they are fused to the labellum in most species of *Zingiber* and absent from *Curcuma graminifolia*. The ovary is trilocular with axile or free-basal placentation. The septation in the ovary may be incomplete in some genera and species. The fruits are fleshy capsules dehiscing either by valves or irregularly.

Fig. 11.4 Zingibereae of Cambodia, Laos and Vietnam (from left to right, top to bottom): *Boesenbergia, Cautleya, Curcuma, Distichochlamys, Hedychium, Kaempferia, Monolophus, Newmania* and *Zingiber*.

KEY TO GENERA IN CAMBODIA, LAOS AND VIETNAM

1. Plane of the leafy shoot perpendicular to the fibrous rhizome, lateral staminodes greatly reduced or, if petaloid, the labellum with green spots and the fruits narrowly cylindrical, like bean pods (Alpinieae) 2

1. Plane of the leafy shoot parallel to the rhizome, lateral staminodes well-developed, petaloid or, if missing, sterile coma bracts present at the top of the inflorescence (Zingibereae & Globbeae) 8

2. Inflorescence arising at the top of the leafy shoot 3
2. Inflorescence arising on a leafless shoot from the rhizome 4

3. Lateral staminodes petaloid, connate to the labellum, labellum white or pale yellow with green patches, fruits narrowly elongate, like bean pods .... *Siliquamomum* (p. 156)
3. Lateral staminodes small, free to base, often narrowly triangular, labellum white or pale yellow, often ornamented by pink or red, fruits globose or slightly elongate, never more than 4 times longer than broad .... *Alpinia* (p. 110)

4. Inflorescence surrounded by an involucre of sterile bracts at base and rachis strongly condensed into a domed receptacle 5
4. Inflorescence not surrounded by involucre of sterile bracts, rachis more or less elongate 6

5. Filament lacking, staminal tube inconspicuous .... *Hornstedtia* (p. 152)
5. Filament present, staminal tube conspicuous .... *Etlingera* (p. 140)

6. Inflorescence lax with clearly visible rachis, bracts caducous, bearing (2–)3–4 flowers .... *Geostachys* (p. 148)
6. Inflorescence usually dense with hidden rachis, bracts persistent or rotting but not caducous, bearing 1 flower (rarely 2–3) 7

7. Leafy shoots composed of one or a few leaves (usually fewer than 5), bracteoles almost always open to the base, floral tube long and slender, anther crest petaloid .... *Elettariopsis* (p. 136)

7. Leafy shoots composed of many leaves (usually more than 5), bracteoles almost always tubular, floral tube short, anther crest trilobed or semilunar .... *Amomum* (p. 122)

8. Filament long, arching over the labellum (Globbeae) 9
8. Filament short or, if long, then straight (Zingibereae) 10

9. Inflorescence borne on leafy shoot, lip bilobed, corolla lobes more or less boat-shaped, never curled backwards .... *Globba* (p. 164)

9. Inflorescence arising before leaves on a leafless shoot, lip trilobed, corolla lobes more or less flat, curled backwards .... *Gagnepainia* (p. 160)

10. Swelling at the base of lamina or petiole (pulvinus) present, anther crest long, curved, wrapped round the style .... *Zingiber* (p. 216)

10. Leaves without swollen petiole, anther crest, if present, not wrapped around the style 11

11. Bracts fused at base to form pouches or free but of two types, fertile bracts and coma bracts .... *Curcuma* (p. 180)

11. Bracts free to base 12

12. Bracts spiral 13

12. Bracts distichous or secund 16

13. Anther with spurs .... *Cautleya* (p. 176)

13. Anther without spurs 14

14. Filament elongate, at least 2 cm long .... *Hedychium* (p. 196)

14. Filament short, no longer than 1 cm 15

15. Slender leafy shoots with well-developed pseudostem, inflorescences always arising from rhizome and always appearing together with leafy shoots, epigynous glands absent .... *Newmania* (p. 212)

15. Leafy shoots composed of two to a few leaves, with poorly developed pseudostem, inflorescences arising between the leaves, or on a separate peduncle before the leafy shoots, epigynous glands present .... *Kaempferia* (p. 202)

16. Flowers opening from top of inflorescence downwards, labellum saccate, white or pale yellow with pink or red markings .... *Boesenbergia* (p. 170)

16. Flowers opening from base of inflorescence upwards, labellum flat, sometimes slightly curved but not saccate, flowers bright yellow, rarely with red markings 17

17. Rhizomes creeping, leafy shoots composed of one or few broadly ovate leaves, labellum deeply bilobed, anther crest lacking or minute, ovary trilocular .... *Distichochlamys* (p. 192)

17. Rhizomes short, leafy shoots forming well-developed but delicate pseudostems, labellum broadly ovate, never deeply bilobed, anther crest petaloid, reflexed, ovary unilocular .... *Monolophus* (p. 208)

CLASSIFICATION

Fig. 12.1 | *Alpinia polyantha,* found in Xuân Sơn National Park is another new record in Vietnam.

Alpinia

Alpinia **Roxb., Asiat. Res. 11: 350. 1810 (nom. cons.)**
Named in honour of Italian botanist Prospero Alpino (1533–1617).
Vernacular names: *krakei, romdeng* (Khmer), *kha* (Lao), *riêng, ré, sẹ*
(Vietnamese), shell ginger, greater galangal (English).

DIAGNOSTIC CHARACTERS

The inflorescence is borne terminally on the leafy stem. The erect inflorescences, flowers often ornamented with red or pink, and lack of well-developed lateral staminodes distinguish *Alpinia* easily from *Siliquamomum*.

DESCRIPTION

Alpinia is a large and diverse genus of small to large clump-forming herbs. The rhizomes are branched, usually positioned on or just below the ground, but can be quite deep in some species. The leafy shoots may be erect or arching, 0.5—3 m tall, usually with many leaves. The ligules are entire or bilobed, usually fairly rigid and not too long, though papery ligules also occur. The petioles are short or missing in some species, but are well-developed in others. The leaf blades vary tremendously in this large genus, from narrowly strap-shaped, narrowly to broadly elliptic, ovate or obovate. They may be smooth, or more or less strongly plicate or rugose. The colour ranges from light to dark green, glossy to velvety matt, with various kinds and degree of hair on one or both sides. The inflorescences are always borne terminally, at the top of the

Fig. 12.2 Flowers of *Alpinia macrostaminodia* have unusually large lateral staminodes. The species was originally described in Thailand and has since been found in Laos.

Fig. 12.3 The variety of flowers in *Alpinia*: *Alpinia conchigera* (upper left), *Alpinia* aff. *latilabris* (upper right), *Alpinia* aff. *strobiliformis* (lower left) and *Alpinia oxymitra* (lower right).

leafy shoots. They are usually erect (rarely drooping), and usually composed of many flowers which appear in cincinni of 1—10 flowers. The rachis is usually simple though it may be branched in a few species. The flowers may be arranged densely and close to the rachis, or on pedicels and spreading. The budding inflorescence is enclosed in a few large sterile bracts which soon drop off. The fertile bracts also often soon fall or,

Fig. 12.4 | The variety of fruit types in *Alpinia*: *Alpinia oblongifolia* (upper left), *Alpinia oxymitra* (upper right), *Alpinia* sp. (lower left) and *Alpinia* aff. *strobilifera* (lower right).

in some species, are missing altogether. The bracteoles, if present, may be open or tubular. The flowers are pedicellate, sometimes very shortly, opening from base to top of the inflorescence. The calyx is tubular, often with two to three teeth and with a unilateral incision, sometimes inflated. The floral tube is usually short and, like the corolla lobes, is mostly white, greenish or yellow, and may be tinged with pink or red.

The dorsal corolla lobe is usually larger than the lateral ones. The labellum is often ovate, it may be entire or with emarginate, incised or deeply bifid apex. The colour is often white and richly ornamented with dark yellow and red patterns but may also be in various shades of greenish, yellow, orange, pink or red with various patterns. The lateral staminodes are greatly reduced, appearing as small tooth-like or needle-like structures at the base of labellum, or absent. Only in a few species are they petaloid. The stamen consists of a well-developed filament and anther. The filament may be stout and as long as the anther, or slender, much longer than the anther. The anther is usually entire, sometimes ending in a small anther crest, or bilobed at the apex without a crest. The epigynous glands are short, composed of two or many lobes, in various shades of cream, ochraceous to yellow-green colour. The ovary is usually

Fig. 12.5 *Alpinia blepharocalyx* is a common species in mountainous areas of northern Vietnam, often seen on slopes along roadsides.

Fig. 12.6 | *Alpinia blepharocalyx.*

Fig. 12.9 | *Alpinia oblongifolia* is commonly seen throughout northern Vietnam.

Fig. 12.10 | *Alpinia velutina* is so far known only from the type locality near Đà Lạt, Vietnam.

Fig. 12.11 | *Alpinia blepharocalyx* var. *glabrior* in Xuân Sơn National Park, northern Vietnam.

Fig. 12.12 | *Alpinia rugosa*, originally described in China, extends southwards to central Vietnam.

Fig. 12.13. | The flowers of *Alpinia maclurei* have very long, arched filaments and are reminiscent of *Globba*.

Fig. 12.14 | *Alpinia calcicola* is a striking species confined to limestone areas of central and northern Vietnam.

Alpinioideae/ ALPINIA

Fig. 13.1 | *Amomum tenellum,* a recently described species from Laos and Vietnam, resembles *Amomum staminidivum* from Borneo.

Amomum

Amomum **Roxb., Pl. Coromandel 3: 75. 1820 (nom. cons.)**
Derived from *amomon*, the Greek name of an Indian spice
plant. Vernacular names: *krevanh* (Khmer), *mak neng* (Lao),
sa nhân, mè tré, thảo quả (Vietnamese), wild cardamom,
false cardamom (English).

DIAGNOSTIC CHARACTERS

The inflorescences are always borne radically. The fertile bracts are persistent, unlike those of *Geostachys*. There is no involucre of sterile bracts, nor a conspicuous tube formed by the base of the filament fusing to the base of the labellum, as found in *Etlingera*. The inflorescence is never fusiform, as in *Hornstedtia*. The leafy shoots are mostly composed of many leaves (usually more than 5), the flowers usually have a short floral tube, the anther crest is trilobed or lunar-shaped and the bracteoles are almost always tubular, differentiating *Amomum* in most cases from *Elettariopsis*.

DESCRIPTION

Amomum is a large and diverse genus of medium-sized to large, clump-forming or spreading herbs. The rhizomes are branched, usually positioned on or just below the ground, but a few species have rhizomes buried deeper in the ground or raised on stilt roots. The leafy shoots may be erect or arching, 1–3.5 m tall, with few to many leaves. The ligules may be thick or thin, papery entire or lobed, the lobes may be short or long, and with blunt or sharp apices. The petioles are short or absent. The leaf blades range from narrowly elliptic to elliptic, ovate or obovate, often slightly leathery and smooth, but may be thin and more or less strongly plicate, mid to dark

Fig. 13.2 | *Amomum elephantorum.*

Fig. 13.3 The shape of the ligules varies greatly in *Amomum* (from left): *Amomum sericeum, Amomum koenigii, Amomum longiligulare,* and *Amomum* aff. *plicatum.*

green, with glossy or matt appearance. Some species have a pretty reddish blush on the undersides of young leaves, while others bear a silvery sheen made of dense, shortly appressed hairs. The inflorescences arise from the rhizome, and consist of a peduncle and few- to many-flowered spike. The peduncles are erect or creeping, usually short, less than 30 cm in length, but may rarely be longer than 1 m. The spikes are broadly ovate, ovate to fusiform in shape. They are composed of loose or dense fertile bracts, which are mostly boat-shaped, narrowly ovate, ovate to narrowly oblong to oblong, usually supporting a single flower. The bracteoles are tubular, with only a few exceptions. The flowers are shortly pedicellate, opening from base to top of the inflorescence. The calyx is tubular, often with two to three teeth and with a unilateral incision. The floral tube is usually short and, like the corolla lobes, is mostly white or yellow, and may be tinged with pink or red. The dorsal corolla lobe is usually larger than the lateral ones. The labellum is mostly clawed or spathulate. It is mostly white, often ornamented with yellow and red patterns, but may also be yellow or light orange with red patterns. The lateral staminodes are greatly reduced to small tooth-like or needle-like structures at the base of labellum, or not visible at all. The stamen consists of a well-developed filament and anther. The filament is usually once to twice the length of anther, but may be shorter. The anther almost always ends in a prominent, variously shaped and often lobed anther crest. There are two epigynous glands, usually quite short, cream or ochraceous. The ovary is cylindrical or globose in shape, trilocular with axile placentation. It can be smooth, verrucose or with faint

Fig. 13.4 The variety of fruit types in *Amomum*: *Amomum koenigii* (upper left), *Amomum sericeum* (upper right), *Amomum villosum* (lower left) and *Amomum* aff. *plicatum* (lower right).

ridges, and it may be glabrous or covered in various kinds of hair. The fruits are thick, fleshy, indehiscent, globose or ovoid capsules, which may be smooth, echinate or with winged ridges. The seeds are dark brown to black when fully ripe, many-angled, fully embedded in a juicy, white to semi-translucent white aril.

Fig. 13.5 | *Amomum putrescens,* a native of China, has only recently been found in Xuân Sơn National Park, northern Vietnam. The inflorescences have long peduncles.

HABITAT
Found from the lowlands to the highlands, mostly in the understorey of deciduous and evergreen forests, often near streams and wet places. Some species are also found in secondary forests, along roadsides and other open or disturbed habitats.

DISTRIBUTION
A large genus with almost 180 species widely distributed in tropical and subtropical Asia. Almost 40 species have so far been recorded from Cambodia, Laos and Vietnam. As new records and new species continue to be reported, the number of species may reach 50.

Fig. 13.6 *Amomum putrescens* is a robust species with shoots 1–3 m tall.

USES & POTENTIAL

The fruits of several *Amomum* species are used as cardamom substitutes, for example, in flavouring soups. *Amomum tsaoko* is cultivated on a large scale in northern Laos and northern Vietnam. In Vietnam, the fruits of various *Amomum* species are pickled for extended periods in locally produced alcohol and the potion is then used to alleviate backaches. Several *Amomum* species are used in Laos in steam saunas and baths.

Fig. 13.7 | *Amomum villosum* (above) and *Amomum microcarpum* (below) are economically important species particularly in Laos, where the fruits are harvested as wild cardamom and exported in large quantities mainly to China, but also to Korea, Thailand and Vietnam.

NOTES

Amomum is another large, very diverse genus which is likely to be split into several smaller genera in the near future.

Fig. 13.8 | *Amomum rubidum* is a recently described species from the Vietnamese side of the Annamite Mountain range. The young leaves have a distinct red blush on the lower side of the leaf blades.

Fig. 13.9 *Amomum* aff. *muricarpum* is commonly encountered in montane forests in Vietnam.

Alpinioideae / AMOMUM

Fig. 13.10 *Amomum dealbatum* has one of the most attractive flowers in the genus.

Alpinioideae / AMOMUM

Fig. 13.11 | *Amomum chinense* occurs in Cambodia, Laos and Vietnam. In Laos, the slightly sweet and acidic fruits are known as *mak sa* and are eaten. The seeds are used for treating toothache.

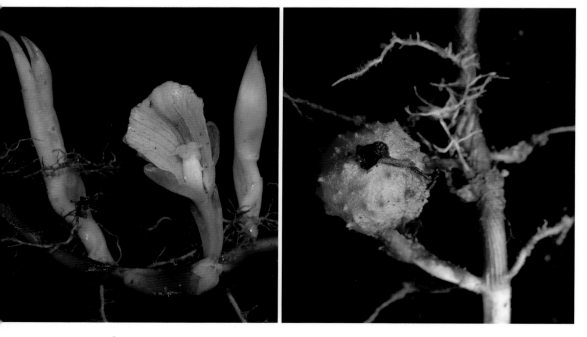

Fig. 13.12 | *Amomum schmidtii* is a fairly common species in Cambodia, Laos and Vietnam, previously identified with *Amomum biflorum* of Peninsular Malaysia and Thailand.

Fig. 13.13 | *Amomum tomrey* is rather similar to *Amomum koenigii* (below), but A. *tomrey* can be recognised by its more globose and hairy fruits and its leaf blades being hairy along the margin.

Fig. 13.14 | *Amomum koenigii* has elliptic, smooth and lenticellate fruits and leaf blades which are glabrous along the margin.

Fig. 13.15 | *Amomum repoeense* is relatively common in lowland to mid-elevation forests and recorded from all three countries.

Fig. 13.16 | *Amomum plicatum* was recently described in Laos and has since been collected several times in Vietnam.

Alpinioideae / AMOMUM

Fig. 13.17 | *Amomum tsaoko* is known to occur in China, Laos and Vietnam. The fruits are usually dark red when ripe and used in traditional medicine.

Fig. 13.18 | *Amomum uliginosum* (left) and *A. longiligulare* (right) are similar to *A. villosum*. *A. uliginosum* differs by having lateral staminodes, while *A. longiligulare* can be recognised by its long ligules.

Fig. 14.1 | *Elettariopsis* species usually form large loose patches.

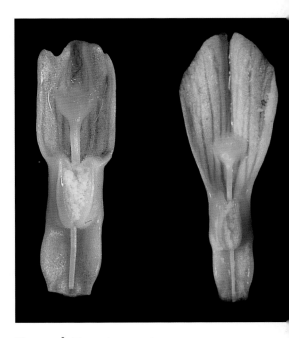

Elettariopsis

Elettariopsis **Baker, in J. D. Hooker, Fl. Brit. India 6: 251. 1892**
Derived from the Latin name of the true cardamom *Elettaria* and
Greek *'opsis'*, meaning appearance. Vernacular names: *khing keng*
(Lao), *tiểu đậu khấu* (Vietnamese).

DIAGNOSTIC CHARACTERS

The inflorescences are always borne radically, and are composed of a few flowers with
long and slender floral tubes. The leafy shoots are usually composed of one or a few
leaves (usually fewer than five), the bracteoles are almost always open to the base,
and the anther crest is petaloid, differentiating *Elettariopsis* from *Geostachys* and in
most cases from *Amomum*.

DESCRIPTION

Elettariopsis species are small to medium-sized
herbs, with slender and creeping rhizomes,
often forming large colonies. The leafy shoots
consist of one to a few leaves, usually fewer
than five. The ligules may be thick or paper-thin,
entire, with blunt or sharp apices. The petioles
may be short or long. The leaf blades range from
narrowly to broadly elliptic, ovate or obovate,
often somewhat leathery and smooth, but may
also be weakly plicate or rugose, mid to dark
green, usually glossy. The leaves are strongly
aromatic when crushed, exhibiting a wide
range of strong spicy scents (e.g. lemon-grass,
cinnamon or less pleasant smells resembling
smelly insects). The inflorescences always
arise directly from the rhizome, and consist
of a peduncle and spike which may be erect
or prostrate. The peduncles are usually short,

Fig. 14.2 | The anther crest in
Elettariopsis is usually
large and petaloid.

Fig. 14.3 | *Elettariopsis 'mirantha'* (left) and *Elettariopsis 'lutescens'* (right) are examples of new species currently being described from Vietnam.

and the spikes few-flowered. The spikes are composed of narrowly ovate to narrowly obovate fertile bracts supporting one flower each. These may be either clustered or spaced along the rachis which may in some species branch. The bracteoles are almost always open to the base (not tubular). The flowers are shortly pedicellate, opening from the base to the top of the inflorescence. The calyx is tubular, with two to three teeth and with a unilateral incision. The floral tube is usually long and slender and, like the corolla lobes, is mostly white or pale yellow or greenish, and may be slightly tinged with pink or red. The dorsal corolla lobe is usually larger than the two lateral ones. The labellum is mostly obovate or rhombic, often three-lobed, usually with a basal claw. It is mostly white, often ornamented with yellow and red patterns at the centre, but may also be yellow with red patterns. The lateral staminodes are greatly reduced to small tooth-like swellings or needle-like structures at the base of labellum, or absent. The stamen consists of a well-developed filament and anther. The filament is usually broad, and as long as or shorter than the anther. The anther mostly ends in a prominent, petaloid anther crest. There are two epigynous glands, slender, with blunt or narrowly acute apices, cream coloured. The ovary is cylindrical or globose, trilocular with axile placentation. It may be fairly smooth or weakly verrucose, often hairy. The fruits are thick, fleshy, indehiscent capsules, which are often ornamented with ridges or blunt warts. The seeds are dark brown to black when fully ripe, many-angled, and fully embedded in a juicy, white to semi-translucent white aril.

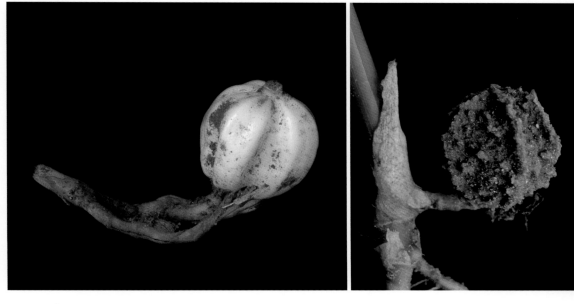

Fig. 14.4 | Fruits of two species of *Elettariopsis*, both from Vietnam, which cannot be identified until flowers are collected.

HABITAT

Found from the lowlands to the highlands, mostly in the understorey of primary deciduous and evergreen forests, often near streams and wet places. Mostly restricted to primary habitats.

DISTRIBUTION

A small genus with about 20 species in SE Asia, of which only three have been formally recognised in Laos and Vietnam. Recent surveys suggest that this number will soon increase.

USES & POTENTIAL

The leaves are used locally for wrapping food, such as sticky rice cakes.

NOTES

Morphology as well as recent molecular studies suggest that *Elettariopsis* is not well distinguished from *Amomum*. Changes in the generic concept of *Elettariopsis* are to be expected in the near future.

Fig. 14.5 | *Elettariopsis* aff. *unifolia*.

Fig. 15.1 | The beautiful *Etlingera elatior*, or torch ginger, is perhaps the best known species of the genus.

Etlingera

Etlingera **Giseke, Prael. Ord. Nat. ad 202, 209. 1792**
Named after German botanist Andreas Ernst Etlinger (1730-1790).
Vernacular names: *mak teua, mak naeng* (Lao), *đa lộc* (Vietnamese),
torch ginger (English).

DIAGNOSTIC CHARACTERS

The inflorescences are always borne radically, have an involucre of tightly overlapping sterile bracts and a rachis condensed into a rather broad, domed receptacle, readily distinguishing *Etlingera* from *Amomum*, *Elettariopsis* and *Geocharis*. The presence of a filament and a more pronounced staminal tube distinguish *Etlingera* from closely related *Hornstedtia*.

DESCRIPTION

Etlingera species are usually large clump-forming herbs with stout, almost woody, branching and often creeping rhizomes positioned on the ground or just below. The leafy shoots are robust, erect and somewhat arching, 1,5—3(—5) m tall, with numerous leaves. The ligules are entire, somewhat unequal, and the petioles are usually short. The leaf blades are narrowly elliptic to elliptic, or weakly ovate-obovate, with a densely hairy margin, clearly visible particularly near the tip, smooth, mid to dark green. The leaves, when crushed, are often aromatic, sometimes rather strongly and not always pleasantly, smelling of petrol in some cases. The inflorescences arise from the rhizomes, near or at a distance from the

Fig. 15.2 | *Etlingera megalocheilos* is commonly encountered in Vietnam.

Fig. 15.3 | The flowers of *Etlingera pavieana*, a species occurring from Thailand to Vietnam, are red or, rarely, orange.

Fig. 15.4 | Infructescence and emerging inflorescence of *Etlingera yunnanensis*.

Alpinioideae/ ETLINGERA

Fig. 15.5 The infructescences of *Etlingera megalocheilos* are always at least partly buried in the ground. Their colour may vary from white to red.

Fig. 15.6 *Etlingera yunnanensis* extends from southern China to northern Laos.

Fig. 15.7 | *Etlingera megalocheilos* thrives in open or partly open spaces, and can be seen along roads.

bases of the pseudostems, and are composed of a spike and peduncle. The peduncles are in some species very short, often with the basal half of the spike embedded in the ground, but may be long and erect in others, holding the spike well above the ground. The spikes are broadly ovate to fusiform in shape. They are composed of an involucre of sterile, leathery and tightly overlapping bracts on the outside and many thinner and narrower fertile bracts inside, each supporting a single flower. The flowers are arranged on an almost flat receptacle (condensed rachis), opening from the edge to the centre of the inflorescence. The calyx is long, tubular, with two to three teeth

Fig. 15.8 | *Etlingera 'poulsenii'* growing along a stream in central Vietnam.

and with a unilateral incision. The floral tube is long and slender, white, cream-white with a pink or red tinge. The corolla lobes, of which the dorsal corolla lobe is slightly larger than the two lateral lobes, are mostly pink or red, but may rarely be white. The staminal (androecial) tube is well-developed and the same colour as the floral tube. The labellum is unequally trilobed, with the margins of the two basal lobes often folded over the anther, the midlobe can be entire or emarginate. It is mostly yellow, orange, dark pink-red or a combination of these, rarely white. There are no lateral staminodes. The stamen consists of a well-developed filament and anther. The

filament is broad, and shorter than the anther. The anther is bilobed at the apex and has no anther crest. The epigynous glands are represented by a single, lobed organ embracing the base of the style, or by two blunt lobes. They are cream to ochraceous and horseshoe-shaped in cross-section. The ovary is cylindrical or globose, trilocular with axile placentation, and often densely hairy. The fruits are thick, fleshy, indehiscent capsules, which are often ornamented with ridges or blunt warts. The seeds are dark brown to black when fully ripe, many-angled, fully embedded in a white to semi-translucent white aril.

Fig. 15.9 | *Etlingera 'poulsenii'.*

HABITAT
Found from the lowlands to the highlands, mostly in the understorey of primary deciduous and evergreen forests, often near streams and wet places, but some species colonise forest edges, roadsides and other open or disturbed habitats.

DISTRIBUTION
A large genus with more than 150 species widely distributed from India throughout SE Asia to the western Pacific Islands. The centre of diversity is in the evergreen equatorial tropics. So far only about 5 species are known to occur in Cambodia, Laos and Vietnam.

USES & POTENTIAL
The leaves are used locally for wrapping food, such as sticky rice cakes.

NOTES
Etlingera elatior, the torch ginger, is widely cultivated throughout the tropics as an ornamental. The strongly aromatic, fennel-scented rhizomes of *Etlingera pavieana* are used in cooking and steam baths.

Fig. 15.10 An almost ripe infructescence of torch ginger, *Etlingera elatior*. The seeds are embedded in a sour sweet tasty aril.

Fig. 16.1 Flower of *Geostachys* aff. *annamensis*.

Geostachys

Geostachys (Baker) Ridl., J. Straits Branch Roy. Asiat. Soc. 32: 157. 1899

Derived from Greek words '*geos*' (Earth) and '*stachys*' (an inflorescence), referring to the inflorescences which arise from the ground. Vernacular names: *đia sa* (Vietnamese).

DIAGNOSTIC CHARACTERS

The inflorescences are always borne radically, and are composed of flowers arranged on a well-developed rachis supported by fertile bracts only (with no involucre of sterile bracts), readily distinguishing *Geostachys* from *Etlingera* and *Hornstedtia*. The fertile bracts are caducous, distinguishing *Geostachys* from *Amomum* and *Elettariopsis*.

DESCRIPTION

Geostachys species are medium-sized to large, clump-forming herbs with rhizomes raised above the ground on thick stilt roots. The leafy shoots are erect or weakly arching, 0.8—2 m tall, with several to about 15 leaves. The ligules are entire or slightly bilobed, somewhat unequal, and the petioles are short. The leaf blades are elliptic or weakly ovate to obovate, mid- to dark green, almost smooth to weakly plicate. The inflorescences arise from the rhizome, and consist of a peduncle and a several- to many-flowered spike. The peduncles are erect or recurved, less than 20 cm in length, covered in overlapping and, towards the top, somewhat inflated, sterile bracts. The spikes are composed of caducous fertile bracts, which each support two to four flowers. The flowers are shortly pedicellate, arranged spirally on the rachis or all leaning towards one side. The flowers open from the

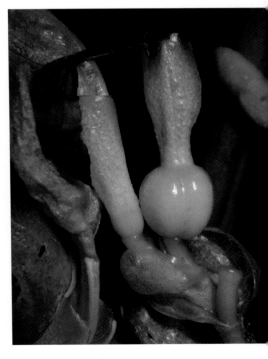

Fig. 16.2 Unripe fruit of *Geostachys annamensis*.

Fig. 16.3 | Flower of *Geostachys annamensis,* side and front view.

Fig. 16.4 | The rhizomes of *Geostachys* species are raised above the ground on thick stilt roots. The space between the stilt roots is often filled with dead leaves and other decomposing organic matter.

base to the top of the inflorescence. The calyx is tubular, often with three teeth (sometimes prominently apiculate) and a unilateral incision. The floral tube is short, only slightly exceeding the calyx and, like the corolla lobes, is white or yellow. The dorsal corolla lobe is larger than the lateral ones, and prominently mucronate. The labellum is connate to the well-developed staminodes, both being white with pink speckles or yellow. The stamen consists of a well-developed filament and anther. The filament is about as long as the anther or slightly shorter. The anther ends in a more or less prominent anther crest. The two epigynous glands are short, with blunt apices, cream to ochraceous. The ovary is ovoid to globose, trilocular with axile placentation and glabrous, or almost so. The fruits are fleshy, indehiscent, globose and smooth capsules, green or purple, with persistent calyx. The seeds are dark brown to black when fully ripe, many-angled, fully embedded in a juicy, semi-translucent white aril.

HABITAT
Restricted to primary montane evergreen forests, at altitudes of 800—1200 m asl.

DISTRIBUTION
More than half the 25 known species occur in Peninsular Malaysia. A few species have been recorded in Sumatra, Borneo and Thailand. Only two species, *Geostachys annamensis* and *G. pierreana* are known to occur in Cambodia, Laos and Vietnam.

USES & POTENTIAL
No uses are recorded. The plants are only rarely encountered in the forests and do not grow in large populations. Although the flowers of some species are strikingly beautiful, it is very difficult to grow them outside the forest environment and to exploit them horticulturally.

Fig. 16.5 | *Geostachys* aff. *annamensis* grows on steep slopes in montane forests of central Vietnam.

Fig. 17.1 | Flowering and fruiting clump of *Hornstedtia sanhan* in central Vietnam.

Hornstedtia

Hornstedtia Retz., Observ. Bot. 6: 18. 1791
Named after Swedish surgeon and naturalist Claes Fredric
Hornstedt (1758-1809). Vernacular name: *sa nhân* (Vietnamese);
spindle ginger (English).

DIAGNOSTIC CHARACTERS

The inflorescences are always borne radically, have an involucre of tightly overlapping sterile bracts and a rachis which is condensed into a flat receptacle, readily distinguishing *Hornstedtia* from *Amomum*, *Elettariopsis* and *Geocharis*. The absence of a filament and less pronounced staminal tube distinguish *Hornstedtia* from the closely related *Etlingera*.

DESCRIPTION

Hornstedtia species are large clump-forming herbs with stout, almost woody, branching rhizomes positioned on the ground or just below. The leafy shoots are robust, erect and somewhat arching, to 3 m tall, with many leaves. The ligules are entire, somewhat unequal, and the petioles short. The leaf blades are elliptic to narrowly elliptic, or weakly ovate to obovate, leathery, mid- to dark green, smooth to weakly plicate. The inflorescences arise from the rhizomes, near the base of the pseudostems, and are composed of a spike and a peduncle. The peduncles in some species are very short, often with the basal half of the spike embedded in the ground, but may be long and erect in others, holding the spike well above the ground. The spikes

Fig. 17.2 | Detail of flower of *Hornstedtia sanhan*, central Vietnam.

are ovate to fusiform in shape. They are composed of an involucre of sterile, white to bright red, leathery and tightly overlapping bracts on the outside and many thinner and narrower fertile bracts inside, each supporting a single flower. The flowers are arranged on a flat receptacle (condensed rachis), opening from the edge to the centre of the inflorescence. The calyx is long, tubular, with two to three teeth and a unilateral incision. The floral tube is long and slender, white, cream-white with pink or red tinge. The corolla lobes, of which the dorsal corolla lobe is slightly larger than the two laterals, are mostly pink or red but may rarely be white. The staminal (androecial) tube is very short and the same colour as the floral tube. The labellum is oblong with somewhat enlarged apex, which may be irregularly laciniate, or bifid, pink, dark pink or almost red, sometimes combined with pure white. There are no lateral staminodes. The stamen lacks a filament. The anther is white or pink-red, bilobed at the apex, and has no anther crest. The epigynous glands are composed of one, two or a few blunt lobes, connate at the base, embracing basal part of the style and horseshoe-shaped in cross-section, cream to ochraceous. The ovary is cylindrical, trilocular with axile placentation, almost glabrous or with sparse long silky hair. The fruit is a subcylindrical or weakly 3-angled, smooth, indehiscent capsule with many seeds. The seeds are dark brown to black when fully ripe, many-angled, completely embedded in a juicy, semi-translucent, white, aromatic, sour-sweet aril.

Fig. 17.3 | *Hornstedtia* species are large and robust plants.

Fig. 17.4 The two *Hornstedtia* species occurring in Vietnam are easy to distinguish as the inflorescences of the undescribed *H. 'bella'* (right) are distinctly pedunculate.

HABITAT

Restricted to primary evergreen forests, at altitudes of 500–1300 m asl.

DISTRIBUTION

Fewer than 40 species are known, distributed in evergreen forests from China to Queensland. Only two species are known to occur in Vietnam, of which only *Hornstedtia sanhan* has been formally described. The genus is very likely to occur also in Cambodia and Laos.

USES & POTENTIAL

The fruits are edible and used locally as medicine.

Fig. 17.5 Ripe fruits of *Hornstedtia sanhan*.

Fig. 18.1 | *Siliquamomum oreodoxa* is the smallest of the three species.

Siliquamomum

Siliquamomum Baill., Bull. Mens. Soc. Linn. Paris 2: 1193. 1895
Derived from Latin '*siliqua*', the pod of a legume, referring to the long
bean-like fruit, combined with *Amomum*, which is a similar genus.
Vernacular name: none recorded.

DIAGNOSTIC CHARACTERS

The inflorescence is borne terminally on the leafy stem. The drooping flowers, with
well-developed lateral staminodes connate to the labellum, characteristic white,
yellow and green colour of the labellum and very long, narrow fruits resembling green
beans distinguish *Siliquamomum* readily from *Alpinia*.

DESCRIPTION

Siliquamomum is a small genus of medium-
sized to large terrestrial herbs, forming
loose clumps. The rhizomes typically have a
blackish-violet tinge externally especially near
the scale scars. The leafy shoots are to 1.5 m
tall, with three to thirteen leaves. The ligules
are about 2—3 mm long and bilobed, often
with a black tinge at the margins. The petioles
can be very short or absent, or to 9 cm long.
The leaf blades are elliptic, ovate or narrowly
elliptic, reaching 45 cm long and 14 cm broad,
with a more or less wavy margin. The surface
is usually mid to dull green, and glabrous on
both sides. The leaves of all species, like the
rhizomes, have a pleasant aromatic scent
when crushed. The inflorescences are always
borne terminally, at the top of the leafy
shoots. They are up to 15 cm long, rather lax
and drooping with cincinni of 1—3 flowers.

Fig. 18.2 The black ligules and leaf sheath margins are typical of all three species.

The lateral staminodes are well developed and connate to the labellum. The stamen consists of a well-developed filament and anther. The anther is usually bilobed at the apex, each lobe ending in an anther crest, which may resemble a small, sharp tooth or a much larger spatula. The two epigynous glands are short and light brown in colour. The ovary is narrowly cylindrical, trilocular (sometimes unilocular at the apex) with axile placentation. The fruits are long narrow capsules which may reach 30 cm in length and resemble long, green bean pods. They open by slits when mature. The seeds, which are to 2.5 cm long, brown with a white to beige aril at the base, are perhaps the largest in the ginger family.

Fig. 18.3 All *Siliquamomum* species have long and slender fruits up to 30 cm long (left). The seeds are among the largest in the family.

Fig. 18.4 *Siliquamomum oreodoxa* (left) is so far known only from central Vietnam, while *S. alcicorne* (right) is endemic to southern Vietnam.

Fig. 18.5 | *Siliquamomum tonkinense* is widespread in northern Vietnam and extends to southern Yunnan in China.

HABITAT
Restricted to primary montane evergreen forests, at altitudes of 600—1800 m asl.

DISTRIBUTION
A small genus with only three species. *Siliquamomum oreodoxa* and *S. alcicorne* have been described recently and are endemic to southern and central Vietnam respectively. *Siliquamomum tonkinense*, originally described from north Vietnam, extends to Yunnan in China.

USES & POTENTIAL
No uses are recorded.

19.1 The inflorescences of *Gagnepainia godefroyi* appear first, before the leafy shoots.

Gagnepainia

Gagnepainia K. Schum., in Engler, Pflanzenr. IV. 46 (Heft 20): 129. 1904
Named after François Gagnepain (1866-1952), botanist at the Muséum national d'histoire naturelle, Paris. Vernacular names: none recorded.

DIAGNOSTIC CHARACTERS

The inflorescence is always borne on a separate, leafless shoot, appearing before the leaves. Bracts and bracteoles are absent, and the orchid-like flowers have a trilobed labellum, of which the central lobe is shaped like a small peg between the two larger lateral lobes. The combination of these characters easily distinguishes *Gagnepainia* not only from related *Globba*, but from any other ginger genus in Cambodia, Laos and Vietnam. The winged petioles allow *Gagnepainia* to be distinguished from *Globba* even when sterile.

DESCRIPTION

Gagnepainia is a very small genus of terrestrial deciduous herbs with short rhizomes and swollen roots often ending in root tubers. The leafy shoots are composed of fewer than 8 leaves, but have a well-developed pseudostem. The leafless sheaths are open to the base and the ligules are very short, barely visible, membranous and shallowly bilobed. The petioles are conspicuously winged. The leaf blades are elliptic to ovate, bright to mid green, and prominently plicate. The inflorescences appear at the beginning of the rainy season on leafless shoots, before the leafy shoots sprout. The peduncle bears a few leafless sheaths. The spike is composed of numerous single flowers, which are spirally arranged around the rachis, and are not supported by any bracts or bracteoles. The flowers are sessile and open from the base to the

Fig. 19.2 | Almost ripe fruits of *Gagnepainia harmandii.*

Fig. 19.3 | Flowers of *Gagnepainia harmandii.*

Fig. 19.4 | *Gagnepainia godefroyi.*

top of the inflorescence. All floral parts are pale orange and white in one species, and bright green with white in the other. The calyx has three clearly visible, narrowly triangular lobes. The floral tube is narrowly cylindrical and only slightly longer than the calyx. The dorsal corolla lobe is only slightly larger than the two laterals, and all three lobes curl tightly backwards soon after the flower opens. The lateral staminodes are well developed and spreading. The labellum is trilobed, broader than long. The side lobes are large, but the middle lobe is short, peg-shaped and a different colour from the rest of the labellum. The stamen consists of a slender filament curved over the labellum, ending in an ovoid, spurless anther which has a small anther crest and no anther appendages. The two epigynous glands are cream coloured, narrowly conical with sharp or blunt apices. The ovary is ovoid to ellipsoid, unilocular with parietal placentation. The fruits are fleshy, ovoid capsules with a persistent calyx, irregularly dehiscing from the base. The seeds are obovoid, bright green, shiny, with a white, irregularly edged aril at their base.

Fig. 19.5 | *Gagnepainia* species have thin, plicate leaves with winged petioles.

HABITAT

Found in the understorey of semi-deciduous forests, usually not far from water.

DISTRIBUTION

Only three species have been described, of which only two are likely to be recognised. The genus occurs in Thailand and Laos, but historical collections indicate that *Gagnepainia* occurs in Cambodia and, perhaps, also in Vietnam, although exact localities are not known.

USES & POTENTIAL

No uses are known, although the two species with pretty, orchid-like flowers are occasionally cultivated as ornamental plants.

Fig. 20.1 Striking, but unidentified *Globba* species from Cambodia, related to *Globba leucantha*.

Globba

Globba L., Mant. pl. 170. 1771
Derived from a vernacular name '*galoba*' used in Amboina Island.
Vernacular names: *kha ling* (Lao), *lôba* (Vietnamese), dancing girl
(English).

DIAGNOSTIC CHARACTERS

The inflorescence is borne at the top of the leafy shoot. The flowers are unmistakeable
with a long-exserted filament, which is curved and ends in an anther with two or
four appendages (except *Globba racemosa*). The style is often stretched across the
filament like the string of a bow. The ovary has parietal placentation.

DESCRIPTION

Globba is a large genus of terrestrial
deciduous herbs with short rhizomes and
swollen roots. The leafy shoots have a well-
developed pseudostem and up to 12 leaves.
The leaf sheaths are open to the base, often
mottled dark red, especially towards the
base. The ligules are membranous, weakly
to prominently bilobed. The leaf blades are
generally sessile, elliptic to ovate, usually
prominently plicate, bright to dark green,
sometimes with a dark red flush beneath.
The inflorescences appear at the top of the
leafy shoots, and can be erect or pendent,
lax or congested, and change appearance
considerably as they develop and age. The
bracts can be persistent or caducous, green
or variously coloured. The bracteoles are
minute, open to base and almost always
caducous. The flowers are pedicellate, and

Fig. 20.2 | *Globba candida* has densely
arranged white persistent bracts.

Fig. 20.3 | *Globba expansa* is a widespread species with remarkably large lateral staminodes.

Fig. 20.4 | The white-flowered variety of a very common species *Globba albiflora* var. *albiflora*.

open from the base to the top of the inflorescence. The floral parts are mostly yellow or orange, rarely white. The calyx is tubular, usually with three more or less apparent teeth, and the slender floral tube curves upwards from it, ending in three corolla lobes. The dorsal corolla lobe is placed behind the filament, while the lateral lobes are positioned at the sides of the labellum. The labellum is cordate or triangular, usually 2-lobed and often has two darker spots on it. The lateral staminodes are petaloid

Fig. 20.5 | *Globba adhaerens* has large but sparse white, violet or green bracts.

Fig. 20.6 | *Globba schomburgkii* is one of the most commonly cultivated species.

and free from the labellum, inserted below the labellum, which is connate with the filament forming a staminodial tube. The stamen consists of a slender filament curved over the labellum, ending in an ovoid, spurless anther. The anther has no crest, but almost always has one or two sharply triangular appendages on each side, except in *Globba racemosa*, which has none. The two epigynous glands are narrowly conical with sharp apices. The ovary is globose, ovoid or ellipsoid, smooth or weakly ribbed,

Fig. 20.7 | Bulbils, which eventually sprout into plantlets, are common in a number of species of *Globba*. They may protrude through the leaf sheaths (left) or appear on the inflorescence.

unilocular with parietal placentation. The fruits are globose or elongate, white or green, fleshy capsules with thin walls. They may be smooth, ribbed or warty, and usually dehisce irregularly exposing the arillate seeds. The seeds are globose to ovoid, usually light to mid brown, with a translucent white, laciniate aril. Many species of *Globba* also produce bulbils, either before the flowers (*Globba racemosa*), at the same time as the flowers, or later in the season. The bulbils, which may be round or elongate, appear in the axils of fertile bracts or protrude through the leaf sheaths, from axillary buds on the true stems. The bulbils can grow into new plants and can be very effective in helping the plant spread vegetatively, even when no seeds are formed.

HABITAT

Globba species are found in a variety of habitats including seasonally deciduous dipterocarp forest, and evergreen broadleaved lowland forest. Some reach higher altitudes in montane forest or pine forest, often near streams. Some species occur in open grasslands, or even in disturbed habitats such as roadside banks.

Fig. 20.8 | *Globba albiflora* var. *aurea* (left) growing on rocky walls near a river; *Globba candida* (right) growing in deciduous dipterocarp forest.

DISTRIBUTION

A large genus of about 100 species widely distributed from Sri Lanka and India, throughout SE Asia to Australia. About 13 species are currently recognised in Cambodia, Laos and Vietnam.

USES & POTENTIAL

Several species with large, coloured bracts have ornamental value. In particular, the species with large white bracts are often used in Buddhist religious rituals. Although medicinal uses have been recorded from other regions, they have not been reported from Cambodia, Laos and Vietnam.

Fig. 20.9 | Unripe fruits of *Globba* sp. (above) and *Globba expansa* (below).

Fig. 21.1 | *Boesenbergia laotica* grows in the open in shallow pockets of soil over rocks.

Boesenbergia

Boesenbergia Kuntze, Rev. Gen. 2: 685. 1891
Named by Otto Kuntze for his sister Clara and her husband Walter
Boesenberg. Vernacular name: *khchiey* (Khmer), *kaxay* (Laos), *ngài*,
bồng nga truật (Vietnamese), Chinese keys, fingerroot (English).

DIAGNOSTIC CHARACTERS

The inflorescences, borne terminally or directly from the rhizome, are often composed
of distichously arranged bracts. The character which distinguishes *Boesenbergia* from
all other Zingiberoideae genera in Cambodia, Laos and Vietnam is that the first flowers
appear at the top of the inflorescence and flowering progresses towards the base. The
flowers are usually white or pale yellow with a spoon-shaped labellum ornamented
with red and/or pink.

DESCRIPTION

Boesenbergia species are small to medium-
sized, mostly deciduous herbs with short
and usually fleshy and aromatic rhizomes,
which are white, pale yellow or orange
internally. The roots are often swollen and
root tubers may also be found. The leafy
shoots, rarely exceeding 70 cm tall, are made
of loose tufts of up to 6 leaves or a mostly
erect pseudostem with up to 10 leaves. True
creeping stems may rarely be observed in
certain evergreen species. In some species,
the leafy shoots die back at the end of the
rainy season, while others remain evergreen
but grow more slowly. The leaf sheaths are
open to base, the ligules are membranous,
entire or bilobed, pale green or translucent
white. The petioles are well developed.

Fig. 21.2 | A spoon-shaped labellum is present in most but not all *Boesenbergia* species (above, *B. kingii*).

Fig. 21.3 | *Boesenbergia* sp. from northern Laos.

The leaf blades are mostly ovate or elliptic, often bright to mid-green, rarely dark green with a velvety appearance, and often prominently plicate. The lower side, which is usually lighter in colour may in some species be flushed red or deep purple. The inflorescence is borne at the top of the leafy shoot in some species (but may be clasped in between the leaf sheaths), or on a leafless shoot directly from rhizome in others. Certain species may produce both types of inflorescence on the same plant. The inflorescence is composed of a very short peduncle (may be negligible), and distichously arranged and densely imbricating, ovate to elliptic, boat-shaped fertile bracts with acute apices. Each fertile bract encloses a single flower supported by an open bracteole. The flowers are sessile, opening from the top to the base of the inflorescence. The calyx is tubular with two or three acute or truncate lobes and a unilateral incision. All flower parts except the labellum are white or pale yellow. The floral tube is long and slender at the base, funnel-shaped at the apex. In some species, a short staminodial tube can be seen. The dorsal corolla lobe is slightly larger than the two lateral ones. The labellum is mostly spoon-shaped, (rarely somewhat flat and with reflexed margin), white or cream white with red and/or pink ornamentation. The lateral staminodes are mostly oblong, free to the base or basally connate to the labellum. The stamen consists of a well-developed filament and a spurless anther which is about as long as, or longer than the filament. The anther crest is either small

Fig. 21.4 | *Boesenbergia burttii* is only known at its type locality, the Bolovens Plateau in Laos.

Zingibereae/ BOESENBERGIA

Fig. 21.5 | *Boesenbergia rotunda*, known as Chinese keys or fingerroot, is cultivated in all three countries but wild forms can be also encountered in semi-deciduous dipterocarp forests.

and often recurved, or absent. The two epigynous glands are cream coloured and usually slender. The ovary is cylindrical to globose, trilocular or incompletely trilocular, with axile placentation. The fruits are subglobose to ovoid capsules which dehisce by three valves that curl outwards, exposing the seeds. The seeds are ovoid to obovoid, light brown to brown or purplish grey, with a white, laciniate aril.

HABITAT
Boesenbergia species are found in various habitats from semi-deciduous dipterocarp forests to humid evergreen forests, mostly from the lowlands to lower montane forest. Some species are confined to limestone.

DISTRIBUTION
A large genus of more than 70 species widely distributed in S and SE Asia, with its centre of diversity in the Indochinese floristic region and Borneo. Only some 10 species are currently known to occur in Cambodia, Laos and Vietnam, but this number will certainly increase.

Fig. 21.6 | *Boesenbergia xiphostachya* is fairly common in southern Vietnam.

USES & POTENTIAL

Boesenbergia rotunda is commonly cultivated and used in local dishes across Asia for its aromatic rhizomes and tuberous roots. In Vietnam it is used in fish soup.

NOTES

Boesenbergia is currently under intensive investigation. The circumscriptions of this and other, closely related genera are likely to change. *Jirawongsea* and some species of *Caulokaempferia* have recently been subsumed under *Boesenbergia*.

Fig. 21.7 | *Boesenbergia alba*, like most of the species previously treated in *Jirawongsea*, has a flat labellum.

Fig. 22.1 *Cautleya gracilis* is a widespread species extending from northern India to northern Vietnam.

Cautleya

Cautleya **Royle ex Hook.f., Mag. 114: ad t. 6991. 1888**
Named in honour of Sir Proby Thomas Cautley (1802-1871), an
English engineer and naturalist who worked in India during the
rule of the East India Company. Vernacular name: *cầu ly*
(Vietnamese).

DIAGNOSTIC CHARACTERS

The inflorescence is borne at the top of the leafy shoot with a well-developed
pseudostem and is composed of a few fertile bracts sparsely arranged around a
visible rachis, each supporting a single yellow flower. The anther is almost L-shaped
with prominent spurs, the anther crest is minute and the bracteoles are missing,
distinguishing *Cautleya* readily from *Monolophus*.

DESCRIPTION

Cautleya is a very small genus of deciduous
plants with a short ovoid rhizome. The leafy
shoots, rarely exceeding 50 cm tall, are
slender and arching, with a well-developed
pseudostem and up to 6 leaves. The leaf
sheaths are tubular, and the ligules short and
weakly bilobed. The leaf blades are sessile
or nearly so, narrowly elliptic, mid to dark
green, somewhat glossy and weakly plicate.
The inflorescence is always borne at the
top of the leafy shoot, composed of only
a few flowers (rarely, only a single flower
appears). The fertile bracts are small, not
exceeding the calyx, and support a single
flower. Bracteoles are missing. The flowers
are sessile, opening from the base to the
top of the inflorescence. The calyx is tubular,
bilobed with a unilateral incision. The floral

Fig. 22.2 The freshly opened fruit of *Cautleya
gracilis* exposes tightly arranged,
black, glossy seeds.

tube, corolla lobes, labellum and staminodes are yellow. The floral tube is slightly longer than the calyx, the dorsal corolla lobe is curved and clasps the two lateral staminodes, while the two lateral corolla lobes support a deeply bilobed labellum. The stamen consists of a well-developed filament and a versatile anther with a minute anther crest and two blunt anther spurs at the base. The two epigynous glands are narrowly conical. The ovary is cylindrical to globose, trilocular with axile placentation. The fruit is a red, globose capsule, which opens upon maturity by three valves that curl outwards, exposing a glossy-black ball-like structure made of tightly arranged seeds. The seeds are small, about 2 mm diameter, black, angular and have a small white aril at the base, visible only when the seeds are pulled apart.

HABITAT

Cautleya thrives in montane forests above 1000 m asl, in wet shaded areas. It may be terrestrial or epiphytic.

Fig. 22.3 | *Cautleya gracilis* with nearly ripe but still unopened fruits.

Fig. 22.4 | *Cautleya gracilis* thrives on wet slopes at high altitudes in Sa Pa, northern Vietnam.

DISTRIBUTION

Only two species and two varieties are currently recognised in *Cautleya*. They are common in the Himalayan region, from northern India and Nepal to southern China, northern Thailand and northern Vietnam. So far only *Cautleya gracilis* has been reported from northern Vietnam.

USES & POTENTIAL

Cautleya species, especially various cultivars of *Cautleya spicata*, are popular as ornamental plants.

Fig. 23.1 | *Curcuma leonidii,* southern Vietnam.

Curcuma

Curcuma L., Sp. Pl. 2. 1753 (nom. cons.)
From the Arabic '*kurkum*' and Hebrew '*karkom*' (yellow), referring
to the deep yellow colour of the rhizome of the true turmeric
(*Curcuma longa* L.) Vernacular names: *romiet* (Khmer), *khimin* (Lao),
nghê, ngải (Vietnamese), hidden ginger, hidden lily, Siam tulip,
turmeric (English).

DIAGNOSTIC CHARACTERS

The inflorescences can be borne from the rhizome, at the top of the leafy shoot, or
break through the leaf sheaths from the pseudostem above ground level. They are
composed of a peduncle and spirally arranged bracts, which are always connate at the
base, forming pouches which enclose usually two or more flowers. The anthers are
always versatile.

DESCRIPTION

Curcuma is a large and diverse genus of
deciduous, terrestrial plants, ranging from
small and delicate to large and robust. The
rhizomes are well developed, fleshy and
generally aromatic, internally white, yellow
or orange, sometimes with a purple, green
or blue hue. In some species they are ovoid,
while in others they may be extensively,
densely branched, with branches short and
stout or slender and creeping. The roots
almost always end in starchy root tubers,
which sustain the plants during the dry
season when the leafy shoot dies back.
The leafy shoots, ranging between 20 cm
and 2 m tall, are usually composed of 2–8
leaves, and have a short pseudostem ending
in a tuft of leaves. Some species appear to
be almost stemless. The leaf sheaths are

Fig. 23.2 | *Curcuma rhabdota* occurs in
Cambodia and Laos.

Fig. 23.3 | *Curcuma pierreana* is easy to recognise by the red-purple tips of its lateral staminodes, though rare individuals in large populations lack this colouring.

open to base, and the ligules are mostly short, membranous, weakly or prominently bilobed. A petiole is present in most species. The leaf blades vary from linear, narrowly to broadly elliptic to ovate, and may be bright to dark green, sometimes with a red patch along the midrib, or rarely with a red flush on the underside. The inflorescence is borne either from the centre of the leafy shoot, or on a leafless shoot directly from the rhizome. Some species may produce inflorescences in both positions. The inflorescence is composed of an erect peduncle, which is for the most part hidden among the leaf sheaths, or covered by leafless sheaths, and a spike. The spike consists of a few to many spirally arranged fertile bracts (rarely only two) which are connate to each other at the base, forming shallow to deep pouches, each subtending two to many flowers. In many species, there are also large, often brightly-coloured sterile bracts, together called the coma, at the top of the inflorescence. Each flower is supported by a triangular or boat-shaped bracteole, which is open to the base but, in some species, bracteoles may be greatly reduced or even missing. The flowers are sessile, opening from the base to the top of the inflorescence. The calyx is tubular, with three teeth at the apex and a unilateral incision. The floral tube may be fairly short and broadly funnel-shaped in the upper part, or slender and cylindrical, widening only a little at the apex. In some species, a short staminodial

Fig. 23.4 *Curcuma corniculata* (upper left), *Curcuma pambrosima* (upper right) and *Curcuma flammea* (below) are some of the recently described species in the new subgenus *Ecomatae*.

Zingibereae/ CURCUMA

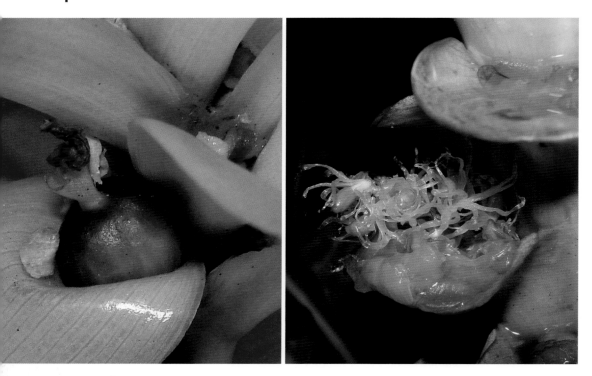

Fig. 23.5 Young fruit of *Curcuma sparganiifolia* (left); freshly dehisced fruit of *Curcuma petiolata* with its arillate seeds fully exposed.

tube can be seen. The dorsal corolla lobe is mucronate and is always larger than the two lateral corolla lobes. The lateral staminodes are well-developed, except in *C. graminifolia*, and may face forwards or splay outwards. The labellum, which is mostly ovate, obovate or rhomboid, may be almost entire with an emarginate apex, or deeply bilobed, sometimes with a basal claw. The floral parts may be white, yellow, orange, red, pink, purple or various combinations of these colours on the staminodes and labellum. A differently coloured central patch, which helps to guide pollinators to the anther (known as the median band), is typical of the labellum. The stamen consists of a well-developed filament and a versatile anther. More than half of the known species have well-developed anther spurs but the others have none. The anther of about half the species also has an anther crest, which is typically quite small. The two epigynous glands are usually cream-coloured, cylindrical with blunt apices. They are present in subgenera *Curcuma* and *Ecomatae* but always lacking in subgenus *Hitcheniopsis*. The ovary is globose to ellipsoid, trilocular with axile placentation. The fruit is a globose, fleshy, thin-walled, white to green, irregularly dehiscing capsule. The seeds, usually less than 5 mm long, are irregularly ovoid to obovoid, light to dark brown, usually shiny, with a white, laciniate aril.

HABITAT

Found in bright, open and semi-open habitats, such as grasslands in dipterocarp forests, or shrubby vegetation on slopes. Only a few species grow in the undergrowth of evergreen forests, usually at its edges. Numerous species are cultivated and some of these easily naturalise in disturbed habitats.

Fig. 23.6 | *Curcuma arida* grows in the driest part of Vietnam, on stony slopes under shrubby vegetation often intermingled with succulent species of *Euphorbia*.

Fig. 23.7 | Semi-deciduous dipterocarp forests are usually very rich in gingers, with several *Curcuma* species often growing together.

DISTRIBUTION

Curcuma is a large genus of more than 130 species distributed throughout S and SE Asia, and extending to southern China, Australia and the south Pacific. Many species are cultivated and naturalised all over the tropics. The highest diversity occurs in monsoonal areas, including Cambodia, Laos and Vietnam, where about 35 species have been recorded so far. The number of species is expected to exceed 40 soon.

Fig. 23.8 | *Curcuma gracillima* (upper left), *Curcuma thorelii* (upper right), *Curcuma harmandii* (lower left) and *Curcuma rhabdota* (lower right) all belong in subgenus *Hitcheniopsis*.

USES & POTENTIAL

Turmeric, derived from the rhizomes of *Curcuma longa*, is the most economically important member of the genus. Several other species with orange rhizomes are used as a turmeric substitute, while at least 10 other species including *Curcuma aeruginosa*, *C. amada*, *C. manga* and *C. zanthorrhiza*, are locally cultivated and traded for medicinal purposes and for use in steam baths. The young inflorescence of species such as *Curcuma pambrosima*, *C. sahuynhensis* and *C. singularis* are boiled or stir-fried as a seasonal vegetable. Edible starch is also extracted from rhizomes and root tubers of several species. Numerous species, including *C. alismatifolia* (known as Siam tulip), *C. petiolata*, *C. roscoeana*, and *C. sparganiifolia* are cultivated for the cut flower industry, mainly in Thailand and therefore have economical potential also in Cambodia, Laos and Vietnam.

NOTES

The species of *Laosanthus* and *Stahlianthus*, some of which occur in Cambodia, Laos and Vietnam, have recently been transferred to *Curcuma*. Molecular phylogenetic studies indicated that these small genera could no longer be maintained.

Fig. 23.9 | *Curcuma singularis* (left) and *Curcuma sahuynhensis* (right) are both consumed as seasonal vegetables.

Fig. 23.10 | *Curcuma sparganiifolia* has great potential as a cut flower and pot plant.

Fig. 23.11 | *Curcuma alismatifolia,* the Siam tulip, is perhaps the best known ornamental species with dozens of cultivars available from nurseries.

Fig. 23.12 | The inflorescences of *Curcuma comosa* emerge before the leaves fully develop. This species has very large and round rhizomes, internally cream-coloured.

Fig. 23.13 | The rhizomes of *Curcuma zanthorrhiza* are bright orange internally and are commonly sold for medicinal purposes.

Fig. 23.14 │ *Curcuma petiolata* is a stately plant and one of the most showy species in Cambodia, Laos and Vietnam. It belongs in subgenus *Curcuma*.

Fig. 23.15 │ *Curcuma plicata* is a highly variable, seed-setting species. There may be a red patch on the leaves or not, a character which varies even within populations.

Fig. 24.1 | *Distichochlamys rubrostriata* can be readily distinguished by the bright red lines on its lateral staminodes.

Distichochlamys

Distichochlamys M.F. Newman, Edinburgh J. Bot. 52: 65. 1995
Derived from Greek words *'distichos'* (in two rows) and *'chlamys'*
(a mantle), referring to the bracts which are arranged in two
rows. Vernacular name: *gừng đen* (Vietnamese).

DIAGNOSTIC CHARACTERS

The inflorescence is composed of fertile bracts arranged in two rows. This character
also occurs in some *Boesenbergia* species but the light to bright yellow, open flowers
with flat labellum which open first at the base of the inflorescence easily distinguish
these two genera.

DESCRIPTION

Distichochlamys species are small, clump-
forming, semi-deciduous plants up to 40 cm
in height. The rhizome is creeping, branched,
white or purple internally, strongly aromatic
of citrol or lemongrass. The roots sometimes
end in fusiform root tubers. The leafy shoots,
which may appear closely clumped together
or loosely, are composed of a single, two or
three leaves per shoot, not forming a distinct
pseudostem. While the plants usually keep
at least a few leaves throughout the year,
growth is severely slowed down during the
cold and drier season and flowering never
occurs at this time. The leaf sheaths are
open to the base and often tinged dark
purple, the ligules are short, weakly bilobed
and wither quickly, visible only on very
young shoots. The leaf blades are unequally
broadly elliptic or ovate, prominently plicate,

Fig. 24.2 | *Distichochlamys benenica,* the most
recent addition to the genus.

Fig. 24.3 *Distichochlamys 'monticola'* (above) and *Distochochlamys 'discolor'* (below), are two among several new species currently being described from Vietnam.

mid to dark green above, and green or dark red beneath. The inflorescences arise from the centre of the leaves or from the leaf sheath when the shoot consists of a single leaf. The inflorescence is composed of a short peduncle and a spike made up of imbricating boat-shaped fertile bracts arranged distichously, each subtending one to three flowers. The bracteoles are tubular, split down one side for about half their length. The flowers are sessile, opening from the base to the top of the inflorescence. The calyx is tubular, bilobed with a unilateral incision reaching up to half its length. The floral tube and corolla lobes are yellow. The labellum is more or less flat, shallowly or deeply bilobed and usually plain yellow, rarely with a red-orange blush in the

Fig. 24.4 | *Distichochlamys citrea* at the type locality in Bạch Mã National Park, Vietnam.

centre. The lateral staminodes are obovate to elliptic, and also yellow in colour, but have a red dot at the base or two red lines in the basal half. The staminodes and labellum are covered in glandular hair. The stamen is yellow, with well-developed filament and spurless anther. A small anther crest is sometimes present. The two epigynous glands are linear and cream-coloured. The ovary is cylindrical to globose, trilocular (sometimes imperfectly) with placentation restricted to the base of the ovary. The fruits are fleshy, ovoid with persistent calyx and are thought to dehisce irregularly. The seeds are irregularly ovoid, with white laciniate aril.

HABITAT
Found in humid tropical evergreen forests, sometimes on limestone.

DISTRIBUTION
Four species of *Distichochlamys* have been described, all from central to northern Vietnam. New species are being described which will extend the range to Laos and may bring the total number to more than ten.

USES & POTENTIAL
The rhizomes, which have a distinctive, pleasant smell and taste resembling lemongrass, are locally harvested and used for medicinal purposes. The genus has great potential for horticulture because of its clump-forming habit, pleasing foliage, beautiful flowers and ease of propagation by rhizome cuttings.

Fig. 25.1 | *Hedychium villosum.*

Hedychium

***Hedychium* J. Koenig, Observ. Bot.: 61. 1779**
Derived from Greek '*hedys*' (sweet) and '*chion*' (snow), referring
to the large, snow-white, sweetly perfumed flowers of *Hedychium
coronarium*. Vernacular names: *sayheun* (Lao), *ngải tiên* (Vietnamese),
butterfly ginger, butterfly lily (English).

DIAGNOSTIC CHARACTERS

Usually robust plants, with well-developed pseudostems. The inflorescences are
borne at the top of the leafy shoots and composed of spirally arranged fertile bracts.
The flowers are well exserted from the bracts, usually with a long and slender floral
tube far exceeding the calyx, narrow and hanging corolla lobes and a well-developed
clawed labellum with a bifid apex. The filament is usually much longer than the
spurless anther which has no crest.

DESCRIPTION

Hedychium is a large genus of terrestrial or
epiphytic deciduous plants with a robust,
sometimes aromatic rhizome. The rhizomes
often preserve the circular bases of former
years' shoots in long rows, and the roots of
the epiphytic species are swollen. The leafy
shoots, reaching 2.5 m in height, always
have a well-developed pseudostem, and are
erect or weakly arching. In most species the
leafy shoot is deciduous, or growth stops
for several months a year. The leaf sheaths
are open to the base, the ligules are well
developed and often papery. The leaf blades
are narrowly elliptic to elliptic, ovate or
obovate, and sessile in most species. They
are mid-green to dark green, smooth or
plicate. The inflorescence is always borne

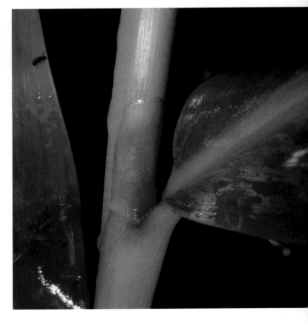

Fig. 25.2 | *Hedychium* species often have long
and thin ligules which soon dry.

Fig. 25.3 | *Hedychium villosum* is a widespread epiphytic species.

at the top of the leafy shoot. The spike is composed of many spirally arranged fertile bracts, which may be broad and imbricating, fully covering the rachis, or narrow, lax and positioned at an acute to almost right-angle to the rachis, exposing much of it. The fertile bracts support one to several flowers, rarely more than five. The bracteoles are tubular. The sessile flowers are well exserted from the bracts, opening from the base to the top of the inflorescence, and the floral parts may be white, yellow, orange or red. Some species have fragrant flowers. The calyx is tubular, with a unilateral incision and small unequal teeth at the apex. The floral tube is usually long and slender, and the corolla lobes are often linear, somewhat curled, with hardly any distinction in shape between the dorsal lobe and the two lateral ones. The lateral staminodes are well-developed, often narrowly unequally obovate. The labellum is bilobed, often deeply so, with a basal claw. In some species, the labellum reaches 7

Fig. 25.4 | *Hedychium coccineum* can be seen in open spaces and along roads.

cm in length and width and resembles the wings of a butterfly, from which the English name derives. The stamen consists of a long filament, and an anther which has neither spurs nor crest. The epigynous glands are narrowly conical with blunt apices, cream to yellow coloured. The ovary is cylindrical, trilocular with axile placentation. The fruits are fleshy, globose, ovoid or ellipsoid capsules, opening by three leathery valves, which are brightly coloured internally. The seeds are irregularly ovoid, bright red with bright red laciniate aril, probably attracting birds.

HABITAT
Often thriving in open to semi-open habitats on slopes and forest edges, sometimes in marshes or on stream banks. The majority of species are terrestrial but a few, usually smaller species, are epiphytes thriving perched on trees or rocks in pockets of humus.

Fig. 25.5 | *Hedychium* aff. *yunnanense* is a common species on Mount Lang Bian in southern Vietnam where it grows in the undergrowth of pine forest.

DISTRIBUTION

Hedychium is a large genus of more than 80 species widely distributed in monsoonal areas from China and India, through Burma, Thailand to Laos and Vietnam, and beyond to the Malesian region. Although some species grow in the lowlands, most are found at higher altitudes, to c. 3000 m. Only about 10 species are known so far to occur in Cambodia, Laos and Vietnam, although more may be found in future.

USES & POTENTIAL

Numerous *Hedychium* species make splendid ornamentals, with *H. coronarium* being commonly cultivated and naturalised throughout the tropics. Commercial breeding by horticulturists has given rise to a great number of cultivars. A few species have been reported to have medicinal properties.

Fig. 25.6 | The flowers of *Hedychium coronarium* open in the late afternoon and remain open overnight until the next day. They emit a strong *Gardenia*-like scent.

Fig. 26.1 Owing to its grass-like leaves, *Kaempferia fallax* is almost impossible to spot unless flowering. The flowers open at dusk and remain open overnight.

Kaempferia

Kaempferia L., Sp. Pl. 2. 1753
Named after German physician and botanist Engelbert
(Englebrecht) Kaempfer (1651–1715). Vernacular names: *prâhs*
(Khmer), *toup moup* (Lao), *thiên liên, địa liên* (Vietnamese),
peacock ginger (English).

DIAGNOSTIC CHARACTERS

Small plants, usually with a poorly developed pseudostem composed of two or a few
spreading leaves, often appressed to the ground. The inflorescences arise between
the leaves, commonly being clasped between the leaf sheaths. The flowers are white,
pink or purple, with a deeply bilobed labellum. The anther crest is well developed and
epigynous glands are present, making *Kaempferia* an easily recognisable genus.

DESCRIPTION

Kaempferia is a medium-sized genus of small
terrestrial deciduous plants rarely reaching
as much as 50 cm in height. The rhizomes
are ovoid to obovoid, branching off in serial
succession. They are white, pale yellow,
purple or deep brown internally and strongly
aromatic. The roots end in fusiform root
tubers. The leafy shoots, rarely exceeding 30
cm tall, are deciduous in all species. They are
composed of a few, rarely more than three,
spreading leaves. The pseudostem is short
or sometimes inconspicuous, and is at least
partly embedded in the ground. The ligules
are short and translucent, weakly bilobed.
Petioles are absent from most species, but well-
developed, for example, in *K. parviflora*. The
leaf blades are usually broadly elliptic, ovate
to orbicular and appressed to the ground, but

Fig. 26.2 | *Kaempferia fallax.*

Fig. 26.3 | *Kaempferia angustifolia* is known as the narrow-leaved peacock ginger.

Fig. 26.4 | *Kaempferia parviflora* is unmistakeable with its petiolate leaves and cup-like inflorescences. Its rhizomes are dark purple-brown internally and are commonly traded.

in some species may be narrowly ovate or even linear, almost grass-like. The upper surface may be plain green or flushed purple, or with white stripes or more elaborate patterns of light green, dark green, bronze and silver-green. The inflorescence almost always arises from between the leaf sheaths, in most species being clasped between them. Only the inflorescences of *K. rotunda* arise before the leaves, directly from the rhizome and can be partly embedded in the ground. The inflorescence is composed of narrowly ovate-elliptic fertile bracts with acute apices. These are spirally arranged around a much condensed rachis, each one subtending a single flower supported by

Fig. 26.5 | *Kaempferia rotunda* can be seen in the wild, but it is also commonly cultivated.

Fig. 26.6 | *Kaempferia marginata* is a widely distributed and highly variable species. Its leaves may be plain green or ornamented.

an open, often bilobed bracteole. The flowers are sessile, opening from the base to the top of the inflorescences though, because the rachis is so condensed, it looks as if the flowers open from the outside towards the centre. The calyx is tubular with three teeth and a unilateral incision. The floral tube and corolla lobes are always white. The floral tube is long and slender, and the dorsal corolla lobe mucronate and slightly larger than the lateral lobes. The labellum is bilobed, and often held flat. Generally, it is white with violet or purple ornamentation, less common are species with white labellum and pale yellow to yellow centre or a uniformly pink labellum. The lateral

Zingibereae/ KAEMPFERIA

Fig. 26.7 | This beautiful *Kaempferia* species, sometimes referred to as *K. laotica* or *K. 'minuta'*, is known to occur in Laos and Thailand. Its identity is not yet clear.

staminodes are large and petaloid, mostly white (rarely pink) and, together with the bifid labellum, often give the impression of a four-petalled flower. The stamen consists of a short filament and spurless anther. The anther crest is mostly large and petaloid, white or pink, entire or lobed, often reflexed. The two epigynous glands are white or cream-white, long and needle-shaped. The ovary is trilocular (sometimes incompletely) with axile placentation. The fruits are similar to those of *Curcuma*, white or greenish, globose to ovoid, thin-walled, fleshy, trilocular indehiscent capsules. The seeds are ovoid or obovoid, somewhat angular, light to dark brown, partly embedded in a white, laciniate aril.

HABITAT

Mostly found in sandy or rocky areas near streams in semi-deciduous forests, and in seasonally flooded grasslands.

DISTRIBUTION

A medium-sized genus of more than 40 species widely distributed in monsoonal tropical Asia. About 14 species are so far recorded from Cambodia, Laos and Vietnam.

USES & POTENTIAL

The rhizomes of *Kaempferia rotunda* and *K. parviflora* are commonly sold at local medicinal plant markets and are often used for relieving backache. The rhizomes of *Kaempferia galanga* are used to spice up local dishes. *Kaempferia* species have high potential as ornamentals owing to their attractively patterned leaves and beautiful white and purple flowers.

Fig. 26.8 | *Kaempferia galanga* (left) is sold as a spice and a medicinal plant, while *Kaempferia pulchra* (right) is often cultivated as an ornamental.

Fig. 27.1 | Gregarious patches of *Monolophus petelotii* flower in July at Sa Pa, northern Vietnam.

Monolophus

Monolophus Delafosse, Guill. & J.Kuhn, Bull. Sci. Nat. Géol.
23, Index: 31, 1830
Derived from Greek '*mono*' (one) and '*lopho*' (crested), the name
refer to the well-developed anther crest. Vernacular name: *đại
bao khuong* (Vietnamese).

DIAGNOSTIC CHARACTERS

Small, delicate plants with a well-developed pseudostem and terminal inflorescence
composed of a few fertile bracts with yellow flowers. The labellum is broadly ovate,
never deeply bilobed, the anthers are spurless and with a well-developed crest, and
the ovary is unilocular, distinguishing *Monolophus* easily from *Cautleya*.

DESCRIPTION

Monolophus is a small genus of delicate
terrestrial and epilithic deciduous plants
with a short rhizome. The leafy shoots, not
exceeding 45 cm tall, are slender, arching,
with a well-developed pseudostem and up to
12 leaves. The leaf sheaths are open to the
base, and the ligules are thin and bilobed.
The sessile leaf blades are narrowly elliptic to
narrowly ovate, ending with a long, narrow,
attenuate tip, mid green and prominently
plicate. The inflorescence is always borne
at the top of the leafy shoot, composed
of only a few fertile bracts (usually fewer
than 10). The fertile bracts may be secund
or distichously arranged, green, narrowly
to broadly ovate with acute tip, supporting
1—3 flowers. The bracteoles are small and
membranous. The flowers are sessile, well
exserted from the bracts, and open from the

Fig.27.2 | The inflorescence of *Monolophus bracteatus*, one of the two Laotian species, has bracts held distinctly to one side.

Fig. 27.3 | The inflorescence of *Monolophus tamdaoensis* bears only one to a few flowers.

Fig. 27.4 | Fully ripe fruits of *Monolophus tamdaoensis* split open exposing a mass of small seeds.

base to the top of the inflorescence. The calyx is tubular and with a unilateral incision. The floral tube, corolla lobes, labellum and staminodes are yellow. The floral tube is long and slender, widening slightly at the apex, the dorsal corolla lobe is slightly larger and shortly mucronate, while the lateral corolla lobes have blunt apices. The lateral staminodes are bright yellow, petaloid, obovate and spreading. The labellum is broadly elliptic to orbicular and usually entire. The stamen consists of a very short filament and a spurless anther, which has a well-developed, strongly reflexed petaloid anther crest. The two epigynous glands may be narrowly conical or very short, almost negligible. The ovary is cylindrical, green, unilocular with free central placentation. The fruits are unilocular ovoid capsules opening by a lateral slit, exposing numerous, small, ellipsoid to ovate, light brown seeds with a minute white aril only at the base of the seed.

HABITAT
Growing in shady damp environments on large rocks near streams, rivers or waterfalls, or in humid evergreen forest, in pockets of soil among rocks, usually at above 1000 m altitude.

DISTRIBUTION
Monolophus is a small genus with 25 species distributed from the eastern Himalayas to Thailand, China, Laos and Vietnam. So far only two species are known to occur in Laos and two in northern Vietnam.

USES & POTENTIAL
No uses have been recorded.

Fig. 27.5 | *Monolophus petelotii.*

Fig. 28.1 | *Newmania* species are fairly hard to spot unless in flower as they tend to grow solitarily and blend well into the surrounding vegetation.

Newmania

Newmania N.S. Lý & Škorničk., Taxon 60(5): 1390. 2011
Named after Mark Fleming Newman (born 1959), ginger specialist at the Royal Botanic Garden Edinburgh. Vernacular names: none recorded.

DIAGNOSTIC CHARACTERS

Plants with well-developed pseudostems composed of leaf sheaths which are tubular at the base. The inflorescences are borne radically and may be creeping or semi-erect on a short peduncle. The flowers are pure white and purple, somewhat similar to those of *Kaempferia*, but the above characters and the lack of epigynous glands make *Newmania* species easy to recognise.

DESCRIPTION

Newmania is a small genus of terrestrial, small to medium sized semi-deciduous plants with short, branched, compact rhizomes. The leafy shoots are quite slender, usually less than 1 m in height, with well-developed pseudostems and 5–15 leaves. The leafless sheaths and leaf sheath bases are tubular, and the ligules are short, to 1 cm in length and obscurely bilobed. The leaf blades are generally sessile or with a short petiole, narrowly elliptic to weakly obovate, smooth or plicate, mid green or greyish green above,

Fig. 28.2 | *Newmania 'cristata'* is one of several new species being described from Vietnam.

sometimes with a red tinge beneath. The inflorescences appear on leafless shoots directly from the rhizome and are either fairly lax and creeping on the ground among the leaf litter or more condensed and upright. The fertile bracts are ovate and enclose a single flower supported by a bracteole, which is sometimes tubular at its base. The

Fig. 28.3 | *Newmania orthostachys* at its type locality in central Vietnam.

Fig. 28.4 | *Newmania serpens*, the type species of the genus, has slender creeping inflorescences.

flowers are sessile, well exserted from the bracts, and open from the base to the top of the inflorescence. The calyx is tubular with a unilateral incision, and has two to three unequal teeth at the apex. All floral parts except the labellum are white. The floral tube is long and slender, the dorsal corolla lobe slightly larger than the two

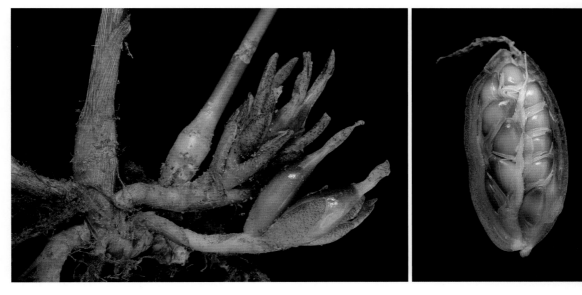

Fig. 28.5 | Almost ripe fruit of *Newmania* sp. with dissected fruit showing the tight arrangement of the arillate seeds. Upon maturity, the capsules dehisce irregularly from the base.

laterals. The lateral staminodes are petaloid, ovate to rhomboid and spreading. The labellum is broadly obovate to cuneate, deeply bilobed, pure violet or with a red patch at the centre and numerous white lines. The stamen consists of a well-developed filament and spurless anther. The anther crest is usually not developed, but has been observed in at least one undescribed species. Epigynous glands are absent. The ovary is cylindrical to ovoid, incompletely trilocular and developing into an ellipsoid to ovoid, purple to dark purple, irregularly dehiscent capsule with persistent calyx. The seeds are irregularly ovate to obovate, deep red to purple with a white, laciniate aril.

HABITAT
Found in the undergrowth of broadleaved evergreen forests, usually in moist and shady areas. The two species so far described occur from 100–500 m asl. New observations suggest that some undescribed species occur above 1000 m asl.

DISTRIBUTION
The genus is endemic in Vietnam. Two species, *N. serpens* and *N. orthostachys*, have been formally described, although more descriptions are under way. The total number of species is likely to reach ten.

USES & POTENTIAL
No uses have been recorded.

Fig. 29.1 *Zingiber laoticum* is distributed from Laos to northern and northeastern Thailand.

Zingiber

Zingiber Mill., Gard. Dict. Abr. ed. 4. 1754 ('Zinziber') (nom. et orth. cons.)
Derived from Sanskrit '*sringavera/singabera*' (horn-root), referring to the shape of the rhizome. Vernacular names: *khnhéi, khnehey, khnhei phlung* (Khmer), *khing* (Lao), *gìrng* (Vietnamese), ginger (English).

DIAGNOSTIC CHARACTERS

The inflorescences composed of spirally arranged bracts can be borne from the rhizome, at the top of the leafy stems, or break through the leaf sheaths from the pseudostem above the ground. Species of *Zingiber* are easily recognized by the unmistakeable beak-shaped anther crest wrapped around the style and stigma (but see also *Cornukaempferia* in Chapter 10). Even when not in flower, the presence of a swelling at the base of the lamina (pulvinus) identifies species to this genus.

DESCRIPTION

Zingiber is a large genus of terrestrial, small to large sized plants. Some species are deciduous, while others are evergreen. The rhizomes are fleshy, branched and often strongly aromatic, cream, yellow, dull orange or purple to violet internally. The roots may end in root tubers. The leafy shoots have a well-developed pseudostem. They may reach to 2 m in height in some species, although most species are less than 1.5 m tall, and are composed of few to as many as 40 leaves. The leafless sheaths are usually open to the base, but may be tubular in a few species. The ligules may be short and fairly thick or papery, thin, entire or lobed, the lobes short or long, usually with blunt apices. The area between the ligule and the lamina is always swollen and is called the pulvinus. The

Fig. 29.2 | The flowers of *Zingiber pellitum* hang down.

Fig. 29.3 | Beak-shaped anther crest wrapped around the style and stigma (left) and presence of pulvinus (right) are two tell-tale characteristics of *Zingiber*.

leaf blades are mostly sessile, only rarely is the petiole conspicuous. The shape of the leaf blade varies greatly from narrowly to broadly elliptic, ovate or weakly obovate. The upper surface may be bright to dark green, rarely with a silvery pattern, smooth or plicate, while the lower surface is usually lighter, or may have a light to dark red or purple flush. The inflorescences are most often borne on a leafless shoot from the rhizome. In a few species the inflorescence appears at the top of the leafy shoot or breaks through the pseudostem above the ground. The inflorescence consists of a peduncle and a few- to many-flowered spike. The peduncle may be nearly absent or very short, in which case the spike may be partly embedded in the ground, or well developed, up to 50 cm long, lying more or less horizontal or upright. The spike is composed of spirally arranged fertile bracts and its shape varies from broadly ovate, cylindrical to narrowly fusiform. The fertile bracts may be loosely or densely imbricate, green, yellow, orange, red or maroon-bronze at first, but mostly turning pink or bright red with age. The fertile bracts usually support single flowers with an open bracteole, but in several species may support two to four flowers. The flowers are sessile and open from the base to the top of the inflorescence. The calyx is tubular with a unilateral incision and one to three lobes at the apex. The floral tube is fairly

Fig. 29.4 | *Zingiber discolor* (upper left); *Zingiber nudicarpum* (upper right); *Zingiber kerrii* (lower left); *Zingiber microcheilum* (lower right) are examples of section *Zingiber*.

Fig. 29.5 The ripe, open fruits of *Zingiber* aff. *teres* (left) simply expose the seeds, while the seeds of *Zingiber collinsii* (right) are embedded in a transparent, mucilaginous liquid.

short, cylindrical at the base but gradually widening towards the apex. The dorsal corolla lobe is always larger than the two lateral corolla lobes, and the colours range from pure white, yellow to bright pink or red. The lateral staminodes are mostly petaloid and usually at least partially connate to the base of the labellum, but species with staminodes almost free to base, and species with much reduced or missing staminodes are also encountered. The shape of the labellum (without the staminodes) ranges from broadly orbicular, ovate, elliptic to obovate and may be entire or bilobed. The colour of the labellum and staminodes ranges from pure white, yellow, pink, red purple to violet and combinations of these colours as spots, streaks and patches on a background colour. The stamen filament is short and may occasionally be almost completely reduced. The anther is spurless and the anther crest wraps around the upper style and stigma, giving it its unmistakeable curved beak shape. There are always two epigynous glands, cream or ochraceous in colour, short or long. The ovary is cylindrical to ovoid, trilocular with axile placentation. The fruits are fleshy, subglobose or ovate, sometimes weakly angular capsules opening by three leathery valves. The seeds are irregularly ovate to obovate, sometimes angled, dark red, purple brown or black, fully or partially embedded in a white laciniate aril.

HABITAT

Found in a wide range of primary habitats including grasslands, semi-deciduous forests, evergreen lowland and montane forests and pine forests. A few species are commonly cultivated and can be found naturalised in various secondary and disturbed habitats.

DISTRIBUTION

A large genus of 100–150 species distributed throughout S and SE Asia, reaching northern Australia. Only 20 species have been recorded in Cambodia, Laos and Vietnam, but the number is expected to at least double as exploration progresses.

USES & POTENTIAL

Zingiber officinale, the common ginger, is one of the most economically important species in the family. It is cultivated throughout the tropics and used as a spice in a wide range of local food preparations such as jams, sweets, curries and various meat and vegetable dishes. Young rhizomes are eaten pickled. Rhizomes of other species, e.g. *Z. montanum*, *Z. zerumbet* and *Z. gramineum*, are important in traditional medicine for the treatment of respiratory and digestive conditions. Although *Zingiber* species are not used as ornamentals in Cambodia, Laos and Vietnam, several species have high horticultural potential.

Fig. 29.6 | Young inflorescences of *Zingiber parishii* var. *phupanense*, known in Laos as *khing pa*, are fried as a seasonal vegetable.

Fig. 29.7 | *Zingiber collinsii* from southern Vietnam has beautifully ornamented leaves, although forms with plain green leaves have also been observed in the wild.

Fig. 29.8 | *Zingiber monophyllum* is only known to occur in northern Vietnam. It is one of only two species in the small section *Pleuranthesis*.

Fig. 29.9 | *Zingiber jiewhoei*, recently described from Laos, has stunning bright red inflorescences and flowers with rich-violet staminodes.

Fig. 29.10 | *Zingiber plicatum* is one of the several new terminally flowering species found in Vietnam.

Fig. 29.11 | Vietnam is particularly rich in terminally flowering species. Some have a hanging inflorescence, e.g. *Zingiber cardiocheilum* (upper left) and *Zingiber pellitum* (upper right) while others have an upright one, *Zingiber mellis* (lower left); *Zingiber nitens* (lower right).

Fig. 29.12 | *Zingiber orbiculatum* (upper left), *Zingiber lecongkietii* (upper right), *Zingiber* aff. *teres* (lower left) and *Zingiber mekongense* (lower right) are examples of section *Cryptanthium*, which is characterised by procumbent peduncles and spikes held at ground level.

Fig. 29.13 | *Zingiber aff. zerumbet.*

Glossary

Adnate. Joined together. This term is used when different parts are joined. Cf. connate.

Anther. The head of the stamen, which bears two small sacs of pollen.

Anther crest. A flap of tissue which grows from the top of the anther.

Apiculate. Having a small, sharp point.

Aril. The fleshy covering of the seed which may cover it completely, or only partially.

Axile placentation. The arrangement of ovules in the ovary in which they are attached to the axis of the ovary.

Bifid. Divided into two.

Bilobed. Divided into two lobes.

Bract. A leaf-like organ on the rachis of the inflorescence, at the base of a cincinnus.

Bracteole. A leaf-like organ on the pedicel of a flower. It may have the pedicel of another flower in its axil.

Bulbil. A small bulb, usually growing in the axil of a bract or bracteole, capable of developing into a new plant.

Caducous. Falling early. This is often used of bracts or bracteoles which fall before or soon after the flowers open.

Calyx. The outer whorl of the perianth.

Capsule. A dry fruit which splits open.

Cincinnus (pl. cincinni). Unit of an inflorescence in which each flower arises in the axil of a bracteole on the stalk of the preceding flower.

Claw. The narrow part at the base of an organ, such as the labellum.

Clump-forming. The leafy shoots growing close together so that the whole plant forms a tight clump.

Connate. Joined together. This term is used when several of the same parts are joined. Cf. adnate.

Corolla lobes. The three free organs at the top of the floral tube, corresponding to petals in other flowers.

Echinate. Spiny.

Elliptic. Narrowing equally towards the top and bottom, with the widest point at the middle.

Emarginate. Having a short nick at the end of an organ, usually used to refer to the labellum of gingers.

Entire. Undivided; this term can be used to describe the end of any organ, such as the ligule or labellum.

Epigynous glands. Glands at the top of the ovary, inside the floral tube. They are probably outgrowths of the walls of the ovary and seem to produce nectar in some species. For this reason, they are sometimes called nectaries.

Exsert. Protrude, stick out.

Filament. The stalk of the stamen.

Floral tube. In gingers, this is the tube made up of the base of the corolla and the stamen and staminodes. These layers cannot be seen, even with a lens, but are thought to be present from morphological studies. In older literature, the term corolla tube was used.

Fusiform. Shaped like an old-fashioned spindle, that is, tapering to both ends.

Involucre. A series of bracts around an inflorescence. These bracts do not bear flowers.

Labellum. The lip of the flower.

Laciniate. Divided into slender lobes.

Lateral staminodes. Two parts of the flower, found at the base of the labellum. They may be as big as the corolla lobes or small, tooth-like or like small cushions, or absent.

Leafy shoot. The aerial shoot of a ginger which bears the leaves. In some genera, the inflorescences occur at the top of these shoots.

Lenticular. Lens-shaped, that is, circular in section and convex on both sides.

Ligule. A small flap of tissue at the join of the leaf sheath and the petiole.

Mucronate. Ending in a short, sharp point.

Oblate. A round shape which is flattened at the poles, such as an orange.

Obovate. Narrowing unequally towards the top and bottom, with the widest point nearer the top.

Ochreous. Light brownish yellow, the colour of ochre.

Ovate. Narrowing unequally towards the top and bottom, with the widest point nearer the bottom.

Parietal placentation. The arrangement of ovules in the ovary in which they are attached to the inner surface of the ovary wall.

Pedicel. The stalk of a flower.

Pedicellate. Having a pedicel.

Petaloid. Like a petal.

Petiole. The stalk which joins the leaf sheath to the leaf blade.

Plicate. Pleated; usually referring to the leaf blade.

Pulvinus. A swelling on the petiole. In gingers it does not seem to function in leaf movement, as it does, for example, in Leguminosae.

Rachis. The principal stem of the inflorescence.

Receptacle. The expanded part of the rachis which bears the flowers. This is only used of highly condensed inflorescences, such as those found in *Etlingera*.

Recurved. Curved outwards and backwards.

Rhizome. A stem which lies on or just under the ground, from which the leafy shoots and inflorescences arise. In gingers, the rhizome often branches, allowing the plant to colonise an area.

Rhombic. Equilateral diamond-shaped.

Rugose. Wrinkled.

Spike. The inflorescence. The strict, botanical meaning of this term is an inflorescence with flowers attached to an unbranched rachis without pedicels. In this, strict sense, spikes are rare in the ginger family but the term can be used more loosely to mean a long, slender inflorescence.

Stamen. The male organ of the flower, consisting of a filament, anther and, sometimes, an anther crest.

Staminal tube. A tube formed of the bases of the filament and staminodes which is longer than the floral tube.

Stilt roots. Stiff, rather straight roots which hold the rhizome above ground level.

Trilocular. Composed of three locules, or chambers.

Verrucose. Warty.

Versatile. Hinged, allowing movement.